WOMANPRAYERS

MARY FORD-GRABOWSKY

WOMANPRAYERS

Prayers by Women
Throughout History
and Around the World

HarperSanFrancisco
A Division of HarperCollinsPublishers

For four generations of women
in my family,
with love and admiration:
Rosa Reissman Grabowsky
Karin Sanders
Sharon Smith and Bianka Wooten
Kasey and Bailey Smith, Shelby and Megan Wooten

WOMANPRAYERS: *Prayers by Women Throughout History and Around the World.*
Copyright © 2003 by Mary Ford-Grabowsky. All rights reserved. Printed in the
United States of America. No part of this book may be used or reproduced in any
manner whatsoever without written permission except in the case of brief quota-
tions embodied in critical articles and reviews. For information address Harper-
Collins Publishers, Inc., 10 East 53rd Street, New York, NY 10022.

HarperCollins books may be purchased for educational, business, or sales promo-
tional use. For information please write: Special Markets Department, Harper-
Collins Publishers, Inc., 10 East 53rd Street, New York, NY 10022.

HarperCollins Web site: http://www.harpercollins.com

HarperCollins®, 📖 ®, and HarperSanFrancisco™ are trademarks of Harper-
Collins Publishers, Inc.

FIRST EDITION

Library of Congress Cataloging-in-Publication Data is available upon request.
ISBN 0–06–008970–9

04 05 06 07 QUE 10 9 8 7 6 5 4 3 2

CONTENTS

CHAPTER 1

Finding Myself 1

[*v*]

CHAPTER 2

The Mother Line 19

CHAPTER 3

Gathering Our Inner Strengths 45

CHAPTER 4

Finding Heaven in Mother Earth 61

CONTENTS

CHAPTER 5

For All Our Needs 75

CONTENTS

CHAPTER 8

Out of Darkness 123

CHAPTER 10

Love 165

THANKS

Boundless thanks to an incomparable agent, Tom Grady, who brings not only professional giftedness to his work, but also grace and integrity.

To the wonderful people at HarperSanFrancisco my deepest possible gratitude, especially John Loudon: a brilliant editor; Kris Ashley: a center of calm and warmth in the writing-publishing maelstrom, a blessing to work with, and Jim Warner: the artist's artist.

And to the outstanding poets and writers who sent me prayers and poems for this book, heartfelt thanks: Sharon Auberle, Karen Benke, Linda S. Boerstler, Janine Canan, Patricia Carlson, Sister Margaret Cessna, H.M., Ruth Fogelman, Barbara Gibson, Maria Cristina Gonzalez, Jeanine Hathaway, Jane Hirshfield, José Hobday, Christina Hutchins, Anne-Marie Madden Irwin, Judy Kroll, Naomi Ruth Lowinsky, Stephanie Marohn, Betty McAfee, Rosemary Partridge, Nita Penfold, Phoebe Phelps, Michelle Lynn Ryan, Regina Sara Ryan, Starhawk, Jan Steckel, Nancy Steinbeck, Maggie Tuteur, Dorothy Walters, Miriam Therese Winter.

To my lifetime partner, Axel L. Grabowsky, my most loving thanks.

INTRODUCTION

A WINDOW ON THE INFINITE

Three years ago, when my daughter was in her final year of medical school, I was casually looking at her medical instruments one day and asked her how to use them. She handed me her ophthalmoscope (for eye examinations), and explained that focussing it is quite difficult at first but eventually I would see a plain white disk in the middle of the eye.

Holding the ophthalmoscope to her eye, I looked through the haze for a long time seeing nothing—then suddenly was amazed by something beautiful and holy. At the center of the eye there was a small sphere of blazing white light, blindingly beautiful. Thousands of sparkling rays flashed in every direction like diamonds, and beyond the diamond light was a glowing bloody background. I felt I was looking into Life itself, seeing the brightest and most beautiful dimensions along with the pain and suffering. A deep insight of the medieval Rhineland mystic, Meister Eckhart, came to mind:

"The eye with which I see God is the eye with which God sees me."

I was literally seeing through the eye into Divine Reality. I knew without doubt that what I had always believed was true, that our lives are grounded in a Life so holy and incomprehensible that no words can convey the awe of a face-to-face encounter. I understood why a scriptural verse says, "You cannot see God and live," while another says that "Moses saw God face to face." Like all mystery and miracles, knowing the Divine is both possible and impossible, the ultimate paradox.

During most of my life, teaching and writing about Divine Mystery, I have carefully avoided using the word "God," resorting to epithets such as "the Ground of Being," "the Wholly Other," the "Holy One," the "Beyond-in-our-Midst." I had taken to heart a suggestion of one of the great religious writers of the twentieth century, Paul Tillich, who wrote at mid-century that we in the West should bury the word "God" for fifty years—and use those years to recover the full meaning of the word. To me this meant reuniting the female aspects of the Divine with the male aspects, bringing the immanent, motherly presence of God into full relationship with fatherly transcendence; recovering our lost women mystics; and restoring to Western civilization the experience of mystical love that three centuries of scientific materialism had suppressed.

Fifty years have now elapsed since Tillich's prophetic remark and "God" is rapidly returning, with a vastly expanded meaning. We now know about the motherhood of God and happily, religions are recovering their lost spiritualities. Four thousand years of sacred writings by women all over the world have been rediscovered and published (as in my book *Sacred Voices*), and mystics of both sexes from East and West have re-educated us about the beauty, joys, and rewards of self-giving love.

MEETING GOD IN THE I.C.U.

Recently, my daughter e-mailed me about an experience in the Intensive Care Unit that shows how even the long-resistant scientific world is meeting God. Here is what she said:

> Friends always ask me, "What is your worst experience as a doctor?" The bloodiest, the most tragic, the most difficult? Strange, this human passion for extremes. But admittedly, my life as a doctor is all about extremes. I walk into people's lives every day. I walk further with them in thirty minutes than most of their loved ones do in a lifetime. I ask about disease, I ask about drugs, I ask about sex, I ask about abuse. Almost everyone answers without question and, I am convinced, without misrepresentation. I have recently started asking them about Faith. I wish that someone would ask me the one question I'd really like to answer: "What is your *holiest* experience as a doctor?"
>
> I could tell them about Clara, an 87-year-old woman I took care of three years ago. She had been healthy all her life, but now her five children took shifts in a round-the-clock vigil by her bed. I remember vividly removing yellow-pink fluid from her lung while her daughter, Elena, held her hand and quietly talked her through all 47 minutes of the procedure, which I'm sure was much longer for Clara than for me.

I saw her every morning before rounds without knowing how much I cared. Perhaps I became too attached, as I wasn't prepared when "code blue, room 137" suddenly sounded overhead. I ran as fast as I could to her room, the sixteenth person on the team to arrive. Although Clara was a "DNR" (Do Not Resuscitate), Elena was screaming: "Do something, do anything, we're not ready, we're not all here." A sister from Mexico hadn't yet arrived.

Clara was in a coma with massive brain damage, fixed and dilated eyes, and no chance of reawakening. But we restarted her heart, then transferred her to the ICU. Her heart stopped three more times before Anna arrived.

One minute after Anna entered Clara's room, she came running back down the corridor calling to the family in the waiting room that Clara had opened her eyes and was writing a note. Doctors and nurses stood with the family transfixed as the impossible occurred. Clara slowly scrawled:

"Take out the tube."

"We can't. You'll die."

"I know."

"Are you sure?"

"I miss Dad. It's my time."

The family heeded her wishes. Afterward, the neurologist told them that he couldn't explain how Clara had woken up. Medically speaking, it shouldn't have happened; we don't have the power.

I have experienced so many holy events in the hospital that it is hard to say which was the holiest. This certainly was one of them.

HOW TO USE THIS BOOK

This book contains 202 of the most beautiful prayers and prayerful poems that I have found in many, many years of searching. They are all by women, and I have gathered them on these pages in the hope that each of them—like my experience with the ophthalmoscope and my daughter's in the ICU—will open a window on the Infinite for you. Their contents celebrate woman's spirit of love and joy; our resilience; our relationships with friends, family, and the wider world; our work; and many of the sacred arts that women enjoy in all cultures and across time—such as prayer-writing, sewing, cooking, peace-making, healing, and consoling. The art of seeing the Unbroken in the broken is presented on every page.

I would like to make a few suggestions for using this book as a powerful prayer-practice. In essence there are three steps:

First, create a sacred space just for prayer in the quietest area of your home where no interruptions will occur and you can have a flower on a table near you, or a candle or incense burning, perhaps a sacred object that you love. Choose a time for the practice as early in the day as possible. Begin by setting a timer for anywhere from five minutes to a half-hour. Have a small pad of paper and a pencil on the table for writing down in a few words any distracting thoughts that come to mind; this way you will be able to let go of mental interruptions. Sit in a comfortable position, then close your eyes while slowly taking three long, deep breaths. Now open the book to the table of contents and select a title that speaks to you, or choose a prayer from a favorite author listed at the back of the book; or simply open the book at random.

Begin to read your selection very slowly, out loud or silently, giving yourself as much time as possible to gently savor and digest every word, every sentence, every verse. Pause frequently to enjoy each image, allowing your imagination to vividly see, hear, or touch one detail after another. For instance, the image of delicious, shining fruit in "This Island, This Season," on pages 70–71, where the sacred is almost palpable:

> Gold peaches
> in glass and plums'
> rich ruby. Black pulp of berries
> thickens in jars.

Visualize the golden light in a ripe peach, the rich ruby light in a plum, the dark light hidden in blackberry preserve; imagine smelling each aroma, tasting the delicious sweetness all winter when snow is piled high outside. You will easily "find heaven in mother earth," sensing how varying degrees of Divine light shine in daily experiences, including the darkest. Now you are on the path of the illumined imagination and will find yourself slowly, gently sinking into the most sacred space in your soul.

Return to the beginning of the prayer and begin reading it again, this time pausing each time you feel inspired or wish to reflect. Perhaps you will find yourself thinking about the long generations of women who have preserved fruit at harvest time. If you wish, write down a word or two that will remind you during the day of the insights you gain during this stage of your practice. Be aware that you are journeying on the truest path to-and-in God; that your body-awakening and mind-opening allows the spirit to enter and penetrate every area of your life, work, and relationships; that you are called every morning to new life, the most abundant life there is.

When you are ready, when you have been with the prayer for enough time and feel complete with it, close your eyes again and spend a few minutes setting the intention of your heart for the day.

You may desire to use this way of praying as preparation for a longer spiritual practice. If so, follow it with silent meditation, chanting, scripture-reading, journalling, or any of the innumerable spiritual practices that the world's great religions have been teaching for millennia. These ancient spiritual practices, like the simple prayer-practice recommended here, are thoroughly tried-and-tested, and will safely lighten your day with faith and tranquillity.*

MARY FORD-GRABOWSKY

---

* Dates of living authors are omitted, and the country of birth is omitted in the case of women born in the United States. The title of Chapter 2, "The Mother Line," is Naomi Lowinsky's name for the generations of women, and the title of Chapter 8, "Out of Darkness," comes from Adriana Diaz. I am deeply grateful to them both.

WOMANPRAYERS

CHAPTER 1

Finding Myself

❋

The Way of the Three Steps:
A Native American Way to Begin the Day

STAND ON MOTHER EARTH. FACE ANY DIRECTION YOU CHOOSE.
(TAKE ONE STEP FORWARD, AS YOU LOOK ABOUT, UP, AND DOWN:)
O Great, Holy Spirit, I take this step into the *day* you have given.
   I embrace all I see—the season, the wind, the fragrances, the
   weather. Let me always accept the day given with a grateful heart.
(TAKE ANOTHER STEP FORWARD.)
O Spirit of Life, I put my arms around *myself,* all that I am, all that I
   can be. I stand here in my own history, with all my mistakes and
   victories. I hold all those I will meet today, in my journeying and in
   my work. I try to walk gently on this earth. Let me walk gently
   through the lives of my work companions and friends. Though they
   make way for my passing, may they spring back, neither broken
   nor bruised.
(TAKE ANOTHER STEP FORWARD.)
O glorious Spirit of Mystery, I put my arms around *you.* I do not
   know what will happen to me today, but I accept it. Give me a

heart of courage and believing, so I may put my trust in you, and
fear nothing.

From the Plains tribes: Native American
Recorded by José Hobday

The Truth About Myself

O God,
help me to believe
the truth about myself—
no matter how beautiful it is!

Macrina Wiederkehr

How Could I Reject Who I Am?

A fish cannot drown in water. A bird cannot fall in the air. Gold is not
dissolved in fire—for there it receives its brilliant sheen. This gift is
given to everything: To live with its own nature. How could I oppose
who I am? I am inclined toward God, and must go through all things
into God.

Mechtild of Magdeburg, *Germany, c.1212–82*

Lord of Healing

Lord of my greatest fear:
Let in your peace.

Lord of my darkest shame:
Let in your grace.

Lord of my oldest grudge:
Let in your forgiveness.

Lord of my deepest anger:
Let in your love.

Lord of my loneliest moment:
Let in your presence.

Lord of my truest self—my all:
Let in your fullness.

Adapted from a prayer by
Alison Pepper, *England*

The Monk Stood Beside a Wheelbarrow

The monk stood Beside a wheelbarrow, weeping.

God or Buddha nowhere to be seen—
these tears were fully human,
bitter, broken,
falling onto the wheelbarrow's rusty side.

They gathered at its bottom,
where the metal drank them in to make more rust.

You cannot know what you do in this life, what you have done.

I saw the weeping monk
and knew I also had a place on this hard earth.

Jane Hirshfield

Listen

Standing in the garden,
left hand laden
with ripe strawberries. The sun

beams off the glassy
backs of flies. Three
birds in the birch tree.

They must have been there
all year.

My mother, my grandmother,
stood like this
in their gardens,

I am 43.
This year I have planted my feet
on this ground

and am practicing
growing up out of my legs
like a tree.

                                    Linda Lancione Moyer

Gestalt at Sixty

I am moving
Toward a new freedom
Born of detachment,
And a sweeter grace—
Learning to let go.

From a poem by May Sarton

———————

Wild longing in my eyes,
I searched for myself
whole days and nights.
Until the Truthful One
found me, right here at home.

Lalleshwari, *Kashmir, fourteenth century*

———————

Prayer

May we reveal our abundance without shame.
May we peel back our sleeping wintery layers
like snakeskins, like the silk chrysalis,

like clothing cast off during love.
May we unravel with abandon like lover's knots
before knitting ourselves back to the heart.
May we settle into our own rhythms as tides do—
within the borders of the moon's calling.
May the music of our souls
be accompanied by grand gestures
and the persistent clapping of hummingbird's wings.

From a prayer by Lisa Colt

———————————

Prelude to *the Dance*

What if it truly doesn't matter what you do but how you do whatever you do?

How would this change what you choose to do with your life?

What if you could be more present and openhearted with each person you met if you were working as a cashier in a corner store, or as a parking lot attendant, than you could if you were doing a job you think is more important?

How would this change how you want to spend your precious time on this earth?

What if your contribution to the world and the fulfillment of your own happiness is not dependant on discovering a better method of prayer or technique of meditation, not dependent upon reading the right book or attending the right seminar, but upon really seeing and deeply appreciating yourself and the world as they are right now?

How would this affect your search for spiritual development?

What if there is no need to change, no need to try to transform yourself into someone who is more compassionate, more present, more loving or wise?

How would this affect all the places in your life where you are endlessly trying to be better?

What if the task is simply to unfold, to become who you already are in your essential nature—gentle, compassionate, and capable of living fully and passionately present?

How would this affect how you feel when you wake up in the morning?

What if who you essentially are right now is all that you are ever going to be?

How would this affect how you feel about your future?

What if the essence of who you are and always have been is enough?

How would this change how you see and feel about your past?

What if the question is not why am I so infrequently the person I really want to be, but why do I so infrequently want to be the person I am?

How would this change what you think you have to learn?

What if becoming who and what we truly are happens not through striving and trying but by recognizing and receiving the people and places and practices that offer us the warmth of encouragement we need to unfold?

How would this shape the choices you make about how to spend today?

What if you knew that the impulse to move in a way that creates beauty in the world will arise from deep within and guide you every time you simply pay attention and wait?

How would this shape your stillness, your movement, your willingness to follow this impulse, to just let go and dance?

Oriah Mountain Dreamer

Grace for My Twenty-Fifth Year

These years, with their open grasses,
have been good to me, have wintered me
and brought me up through spring.
The oak trees are continuous
in reaching into sun.
The golden bowls of harvesting I bring.
I am living in the echo
of a clear bell's ring.

Maggie Tuteur

———————————

Handicaps

I thank God
For my handicaps,
For, through them,
I have found myself,
My work,
And my God.

Helen Keller, *1880–1968*

The Well

It was on dark nights of deep sleep
that I dreamed the most, sunk in the well,
and woke rested, and if not beautiful,
filled with some other power.

From a poem by
Denise Levertov, *England, 1923–98*

Order of Melchizedek

Know who you are.
Do not debase the name.
Carry it in your heart,
a root flame of love.
Walk through the world in silence.
The moment will come.
The sign will be a soft stirring of wings,
a gold shimmer of air.

Dorothy Walters

Bonsai

One morning beginning to notice
which thoughts pull the spirit out of the body, which return it.
How quietly the abandoned body keens,
like a bonsai maple surrounded by her dropped leaves.
Rain or objects call the forgotten back:
the droplets' placid girth and weight; the dresser's lack of ambition.
How strange it is that longing, too, becomes a small green bud,
thickening the vacant branch-length in early March.

Jane Hirshfield

I Was Obsessed

I used to worship
the sun and the moon,
adore gods,
and shave my head.
I took vows,
and fasted after dark.
I was obsessed with
make-up and finery,
jewelry and fragances.
And then faith came.

Now I see life
as it really is.
Freed from all that binds,
my heart is still.

Nandutarra, *India,*
sixth to third centuries B.C.E.

Our deepest fear
is not that we are inadequate.
Our deepest fear
is that we are powerful beyond measure.
It is our light,
not our darkness,
that most frightens us....

[P]laying small doesn't serve the world.
There's nothing enlightened about shrinking
so that other people
won't feel insecure around you.

We were born to make manifest
the glory of God within us.
It's not just in some of us;
it's in everyone.

[13]

And as we let our light shine,
    we unconsciously give other people
    permission to do the same.
As we are liberated from our own fear,
    our presence automatically liberates others.

From a prayer by
Marianne Williamson

————————————

Lord, not you,
It is I who am absent.

Denise Levertov,
England, 1923–98

————————————

Blessed Are You

I.

Blessed
are you
woman of strength
wrapped around
order and chaos
holding firm

tension's pieces
forging new dreams
and promised tomorrows.

II.

Blessed are you
woman of passion
rooted deep
standing tall
touching all you reach
transforming
the heart of
the universe.

III.

Blessed are you
woman of the earth
sculpted from its clay
and fired by
the very breath of God
forming and firing
new life
reflecting

the One who
calls you by name

IV.

Blessed are you
tender woman
freely sharing
laughter and tears
cleansing and healing
weaving harmony
welcoming all
who touch your face.

V.

Blessed are you
woman of wisdom
enfolding, unfolding
mystery and myth
revealing truth and light
for all who yearn
to call themselves free.

Margaret Cessna, H.M.

Be Who You Are

Be who you are,
and may you be blessed
in all that you are.

Adapted from a prayer
by Marcia Falk

———————————

It is by seeking
to know one's
Self
that the Mother of all
may be found.

Anandamayi Ma, *India, 1896–1982*

O Lord,
One tiny bit of water rests on the palm of my hand.
I bring it to you and with it I bring the whole ocean.
This tiny drop has the power to ease the burning thirst of men;
when spread on the earth, to give life to the seed and the future harvest;
when poured on the fire to quench the blaze.
A tiny drop of water
can cleanse the whole of my impurity when blessed by your
forgiveness.

But, O Lord,
more than all this, this tiny drop of water passed over my head
is the symbol of my birth in You.

Ishpriya, RSCJ

CHAPTER 2

The Mother Line

❁

Pastoral

Like an otter, but warm,
she latched onto the shadowy tip
and I watched, diminished
by those amazing gulps. Finished
she let her head loll, eyes
unfocused and large: milk-drunk.

I liked afterwards best, lying
outside on a quilt, her new skin
spread out like meringue. I felt then
what a young man must feel
with his first love asleep on his breast;
desire, and the freedom to imagine it.

Rita Dove

The Boston School of Cooking Cookbook

This is my mother's cookbook, its spine loose
with age, the fabric bare of colour at the seams
and weak, so it must be held tenderly, the way
my mother knows, easing into its pages
with her disobedient-knuckled hands.

This book is my mother's; she navigates
its mysteries with indifferent skill,
reads the runes of food-stains,
the faded trail of silverfish
who ate their random way over words;
she has the eye to decipher the tastes
of another time, scrawled
in the margins, invoking the power
of other kitchens, the fit of old aprons,
the shape of a family
swallowed into other lives.

This book's pages, furred with use,
fade to brown. Its leaves have pressed
my mother's memories in perfect squares, the things
she needs concealed from time,
things she likes to come upon by chance:

household tips and obituaries, invitations
to weddings. My first poem is in there, and the card
someone made for mother's day. Sentiment
among the weeds of recipes she clipped
in more ambitious days
that crowd, untasted, between the even rows
of meals we chewed our way through
but never knew the names of, all those years'
worth of peeled vegetables and trimmed meat,
a lifetime's preparation vanished
into our waiting mouths.

Rhona McAdam

I Have So Much I Can Teach Her

I have so much I can teach her
And pull out of her.
I would say you might encounter defeats
But you must never be defeated.
I would teach her to love a lot.
Laugh a lot at the silliest things
And be very serious.
I would teach her to love life,
I could do that.

Adapted from a poem by
Maya Angelou

––––––––––––––

The Meaning of Bones

Twins of grief—
the mothers of the disappeared
march two by two
on the Plaza de Mayo.
They wear placard-sized photos
of Luis, Claudio, and Lila
as necklaces

to remind the world
of their invisible children.

From a poem by
Megan Sexton

The Tablecloth

On company nights when wine
was poured, candlelight gathered and played
the water and wine, throwing its soul
to be carried
as only liquid and human faces
can carry light;
and laughter played back,
pushing joy at fire
until the flames sputtered and squatted,

                                                    danced

and steadied above the crowded table.

On company nights
long before the candles were lit,
before dishes clinked and chimed,
I crouched under the table

in a calm span of late sun reaching.
My mother unfolded the cloth
and floated it over the table,
embrace and release all in one fluid

                                sweep

of deep red linen. And I loved her,

loved her wide motion
and loved the laughter
late, as I drifted down to sleep
singing whispers in my child's bed,
loved the moments as much as I
would ever love any moments
beside any lover in any darkness
slashed through with quick

                        laughter,

voices layered
and flecked with swaying light.

And now I know that unfolding,
know in my body
the single motion
of welcome and release,
know the tenor and flare of the cloth

                              billowing,

settling smooth, ready for light,
liquid, laughter, draping
thighs and feet and hands and
knees in the tangled dark.

Christina Hutchins

———————

Dying at 31

Padre,
my mother will be alone.
Please comfort her
when I am gone.

Rose of Lima, *Peru*,
1586–1617

———————

Source

My mother showed me.
She pulled a carrot
right up out of the ground
before my eyes.
She ran it under
the garden tap

and held it out to me,
still warm from the earth.

My baby teeth tested
its crisp, giving body.

In that one gesture,
my mother on her knees in Ohio.

Maggie Tuteur

Oh, God, thank you for the child I carry... I walk the world in wonder. I see it through new eyes. All is changed, subtly but singingly different. The beauty of sunlight upon the grass, the feel of its warmth along my arms. It is cradling me in tenderness as I shall cradle this child one day. I am mother and child in one, new as a child myself.

Marjorie Holmes

To Jacqueline, Age 2,
in Her Great-Grandmother's House

Your great grand-grandmother
is no place now,
but I still see her image
in this oval mirror;
she is letting her silver hair down
around her shoulders
like a cloud.

Your grandmother sees her
as a young woman
in an apron,
pinning back brown curls on washday morning.

I see all of us
in your piercing eyes.

From a poem by
Kathleen Norris

Cost of Living

At the check out counter
in Flanagan's Grocery Store,
I tuck stray hair behind my ear,
run my eyes over the basket.

A girl with perfect nails
slides necessities across the scanner:
juice, cookies for school lunch
milk, bread, toilet paper.
Amounts beep and flash,
the numbers mocking me.

I hand her a wadded twenty,
ask for the change in quarters
thank her with a smile I don't feel.
Tomorrow you turn fourteen,
I've enough left to do the laundry.

                              Ann-Marie Madden Irwin

Prayer for Easy Labor

Mother of the Universe and all Universal Knowledge, . . .
Eve, the crown of Your creation, . . .
delivered her children with strength. . . .
May I be infused with Eve's birthing powers.
Let my labor be only mild pangs of discomfort,
Yet may I labor for the revelation of Your presence in the world.

Primal EarthMother Eve tended and cared for Your garden
As I will care for my child.
May this child grow to be conscious
Of your world and environment as Eve did.
Let this child blossom as a garden blooms in the springtime.

From a prayer by
Rabbi Geela Rayzel Raphael

Consecration

I was thirteen when I gave my mother
a small wicker basket of talcum powders,
bath gel and rosewater. Handling each bottle
like a semi-precious stone, she placed them on
the bathroom counter like an altar-offering.

Ashamed of my own body, I was the moon, wanting
to show myself only when the world was black.
I watched her undress and saw her familiar body.
A thick pink scar stretched across
the place where her left breast should have been.

She filled the sink with warm soapy waters,
drowning a sponge until it was heavy with water,
then rubbed her skin clean, sprinkled and smoothed
my gifts onto her body, anointing and preparing herself.

I do not remember if we ever spoke.
I knew only the touch of light on our bodies.

Andrea O'Brien

35/10

Brushing out my daughter's dark
silken hair before the mirror
I see the gray gleaming on my head,
the silver-haired servant behind her. Why is it
just as we begin to go
they begin to arrive, the fold in my neck
clarifying as the fine bones of her

hips sharpen? As my skin shows
its dry pitting, she opens like a small
pale flower on the tip of a cactus,
as my last chances to bear a child
are falling through my body, the duds among them,
her full purse of eggs, round and
firm as hard-boiled yolks, is about
to snap its clasp. I brush her tangled
fragrant hair at bedtime. It's an old
story—the oldest we have on our planet—
the story of replacement.

Sharon Olds

---

to dance at your daughter's wedding

is to be poured
into a cauldron
of liquid ingredient
in some old recipe
a big spoon is stirring you
your former brothers-
in-law your beautiful nieces
from the other side
of broken marriages—

you're kissing the unkissable
ex-husband's second wife's mother—
your new son-in-law's
five year old niece
from texas shows off
her white cowboy boots
with fringe—
in yiddish there's a word for this:
'the machitonem'—
even your other
daughter's man
(the one who won't commit)
asks you to dance
the great spoon is mixing it all up—
your mother your dead
father your daughter in her shining
gown her green eyes
the whole gorgeous ferment
of stirring bodies—
suddenly an agitation among her
brothers-in-law with chairs
the bride and groom are lifted—

                    above us—

her silken tent of skirts
his laughing eyes

our clapping hands
the white linen napkin

held

between them—

Naomi Ruth Lowinsky

_____

Gift from My Mother

I hear the gentle music
My mother used to play
On the grand piano downstairs
As I was falling asleep

The song would leave the piano
At the far end of the living room
Curl around the wall
Into the hall
Climb up the stairs

And slip under my bedroom door
Without knocking

Once in my lavender room
It would wrap itself around me
Like an extra cover
For the night

And I would fall asleep
In its comforting chords
For the rest of my life

Betty McAfee

———————————

Your Clothes

Of course they are empty shells, without hope of animation.
Of course they are artifacts.

Even if my sister and I should wear some,
or if we give others away.

they will always be your clothes without you,
as we will always be your daughters without you.

Judy Kroll

To Elvira, My Maternal Grandmother

You're in the photo, surely,
though only your gaze shows
like the ragged rim of dusk
as you squat behind your daughters,
way behind your daughters,
their dress-up lace and
the innocent dismay of their faces,
as though perhaps you don't exist,
as though you're holding them out
as a shield against the relentless sway
of childbearing that eventually
bled you to death. I cannot
take your hand there. I cannot
even see your hand: only
my own holding your picture,
the raw chaos of my care
for you barely at bay.

Patricia Carlson

The Turning Point

I watch my daughter at her dressage lesson.
Technique and confidence override
metaphor. And I, separate observer,
cannot ever know how
such a brave, slim beauty
will one day assume control, take up
those reins in her quiet hands, and ride
through field and forest, dark water and city.
How a girl outgrows the high fence
of a sandy, soft arena, outgrows the fear
of open space and its thousand ways
she and that horse could go.

How one afternoon when the wind riffles through
my hair, thoughts aloft and balmy,
my maternal arms resting heavy on the gates—
that will be the afternoon she decides to open them
and asks me to step back to safety.
There, I am brought up to the point
of so many lessons. What can I do but nod
in recognition of all that might be sent sprawling?
What can I do but swing wide those gates,
walk back to the barn for a mount of my own?

Jeanine Hathaway

What Came to Me

I took the last
dusty piece of china
out of the barrel.
It was your gravy boat,
with a hard, brown
drop of gravy still
on the porcelain lip.
I grieved for you then
as I never had before.

Source unknown

The Power in My Mother's Arms

There must be rituals
that sever what harms
our connection to the past and lets us
keep the rest.

From a poem by Florence Weinberger

Chains of Fire

I know myself linked by chains of fire
to every woman who has kept a hearth. In the resinous smoke
I smell hut, castle, cave,
Mansion and hovel,
See in the shifting flame my mother
and grandmothers out over the world.

From a poem by Elsa Gidlow

———————

Mother of Mothers

At Mesa Verde Dan picked up a potsherd.
He showed me the pattern of ridges made
by a human thumb. Giving the shard to me
to hold he asked: "Who made this?"

I.

Touching what her hand made
eight hundred years ago
a woman
like my mother, like myself

I feel her sitting
in my bones, turning
and turning her pot
her thumb
rhythmic.

How firmly planted
in her circle of ground she is
       like the Yucca
her thoughts are
as spiny and as practical.

Only for moments in the darkness of the Kiwa
in the unknown of her womb
       does she

Mother of Mothers

allow her fear to bloom.
What will be born
and what will die
in the next turn of the seasons
in the next round of her thumb?

Has too much been taken
not enough returned?
What dark erosion
mushrooms in her dreams?

II.

In my mother's kitchen I am
kitchen table height
watching her thumb
turning and turning
           the knife
           rounds
of cucumber slip into
the bowl like
           pale moons.
She has survived
so many deaths
           and fragmentations

fear lives in our house
like a visiting relative
           who talks too much.

III.

They called it Trinity
as though to harness
the power of the latest
                gods
inhabiting the land

and on the sacred red
New Mexican earth
                they worked
                their miracle:

transformed matter
into energy
smashed the atom
smashed the Axis
made mushroom clouds to bloom
                over the desert

My mother's broken people
                rejoiced
                until
                the wind shifted.

Some
down to earth
     woman

     lost her baby
and began counting

     miscarriages
     still births
     monstrous foetuses, deaths

     from cancer
     in every family
     people wondered:

Whose gods are angry? . . .

     V.

This is the faith I seek:
that in the great round
     of worlds
when I've been gone
     eight centuries

a baby will be born

a daughter of daughters

She'll grow into a woman
        like my daughters
        like myself.

And if I could believe
her time will come
        I'd leave

        her all the world
and all the treasure
        of my life

long crumbled in the dust
be hers to find

to hold within her hand
some fragment of
        my kitchen

by which she'd know
      the ancient ones

have held her

    sacred.

                Naomi Ruth Lowinsky

CHAPTER 3

Gathering Our Inner Strengths

❋

Letting Go

Let go of the place that holds,
Let go of the place that flinches,
Let go of the place that controls,
Let go of the place that fears.
Just let the ground support me.
Listen, the wind is breathing in the trees.
Sensing the edge of soft and hard,
I follow the unseen path.
Walking in the dark night,
I practice faith,
Building confidence in the unknown.
Walking in the dark night,
I practice courage,
accepting the vastness
of what I cannot see.

From a poem by
Stephanie Kaza

A Cedary Fragrance

Even now,
decades after,
I wash my face with cold water—

Not for discipline,
nor memory,
nor the icy, awakening slap,

but to practice
choosing
to make the unwanted wanted.

Jane Hirshfield

Self-Giving

We possess nothing in the world—a mere chance can strip us of everything—except the power to say "I." And that is what we have to give to God. In other words: Ourselves. There is absolutely no other free act that is given us to achieve—only the gift of oneself.

Simone Weil, *France, 1909–43*

Three times each day
I invoke your name in prayer.

Andal, *India, eighth century*

———————

From Self-Consciousness to Happiness

By keeping a diary of what made me happy,
I had discovered that happiness came
when I was most widely aware.
So I had finally come to the conclusion
that my task
was to become more and more aware,
more and more understanding
with an understanding
that was not at all the same thing
as intellectual comprehension.
And, by finding that,
in order to be more and more aware
I had to be more and more still,
I had not only come to see
through my own eyes,
instead of at second hand,
I had also finally come to discover
what was my way of escape

[47]

from the imprisoning island of my own
self-consciousness.

Marion Milner

Learning to Grow

Lord Jesus, Rabbi, Teacher,
thank you for reminding us
that until we bring you our darkness
    we cannot know your light;
that until we become the servants of truth
    we cannot become wise leaders;
that until we are good listeners
    we cannot speak with authority;
that until we become willing, lifelong learners
    we cannot teach with insight or enthusiasm;
that until we are ready to be reborn
    we cannot truly mature.

Kate Compston

May you be drenched with the longing for peace,
and make justice blossom on earth.

Hildegard of Bingen, *Germany, 1098–1179*

The Last Story

And so the time comes when all the people of the earth
    can bring their gifts to the fire
    and look into each other's faces
    unafraid

Breathe deep
Feel the sacred well that is your own breath, and look
    look at that circle
See us come from every direction
    from the four quarters of the earth
See the lines that stretch to the horizon
    the procession, the gifts borne
    see us feed the fire
Feel the earth's life renewed
And the circle is complete again
    and the medicine wheel is formed anew
    and the knowledge within each one of us
    made whole
Feel the great turning, feel the change
    the new life runs through your blood like fire
    and all of nature rises with it
    greening, burgeoning, bursting into flower....

This is the story we like to tell ourselves
In the night
When the labor is too hard, and goes on too long
When the fire seems nothing but dying embers winking
    out
We say we remember
    a time when we were free
We say
    that we are free, still, and always
And the pain we feel
    is that of labor
And the cries we hear
    are those of birth

And so you come to the fire
    where the old ones sit
You are young
    just on the edge of ripening
They are ancient
    their faces lined
    with spiderwebs of wrinkle
Their faces brown, bronze, cream, black
    their eyes are wells of memory
They say
Listen child

For this is your night of passage
And it is time to learn
Your history
Tonight you will run free, out into the wild
Fearing only the spirit of your own power
And no one in this world would harm you or lay
    a hand on you
But there was a time
When children were not safe

                                            Starhawk

———————————

As I light these Sabbath candles
Gracious Creator
I thank you for these past seven days.
Thank you for protecting my family
and bringing us safely through the week;
for deeper understanding of each other;
for strengthening one another
by sharing our joys and disappointments
our victories and mistakes.
I pray that in this coming week
Our pride in one another and our love
will grow, that we will have good health
and you will be with us

[51]

and with everyone everywhere
who feels lost or threatened or ill.

Adapted from a traditional Jewish prayer

In Pain

God spoke to me:
Trust me and follow my words in all things;
However long you are ill, I will care for you.
All those things which you need in body and soul
I will give to you.

Mechtild of Magdeburg, *Germany, c.1212–82*

Buddhist Vow

Knowing how deeply our lives intertwine,
We vow not to kill.

Knowing how deeply our lives intertwine,
We vow to not take what is not given.

Knowing how deeply our lives intertwine,
We vow to not engage in abusive relationships.

Knowing how deeply our lives intertwine,
We vow to not speak falsely or deceptively.

Knowing how deeply our lives intertwine,
We vow to not harm self or other through
poisonous thought or substance.

Knowing how deeply our lives intertwine,
We vow to not dwell on past errors.

Knowing how deeply our lives intertwine,
We vow to not possess any thing or form of life
selfishly.

Knowing how deeply our lives intertwine,
We vow to not harbor ill will toward any plant, animal, or
human being.

Knowing how deeply our lives intertwine,
We vow to not abuse the great truth of the Three
Treasures.*

Stephanie Kaza

In Buddhism, the Three Treasures refer to the Buddha, the dharma (teachings), and the sangha (community).

Moments of Real Grace

Sometimes, during my early-morning meditation, a place within me opens and parts of myself let go that I did not even know were holding on. In these moments I feel all the hard parts in my heart and body yield to a great softness carried on my breath, . . .

A great faith washes through me, a knowing that everything that needs to get done will get done. My shoulders drop an inch, the small but familiar ache in my chest eases, and the moment stretches. There is enough: enough time, enough energy, enough of all that is needed. A great tenderness for myself and the world opens inside me, and I know I belong to this time, to these people, to this earth, and to something that is both within and larger than all of it, something that sustains and holds us all. I do not want to be anywhere else. I am filled with commitment . . . and compassion.

Oriah Mountain Dreamer

Life in Ravensbruck*

Life in Ravensbruck,
unfolding on two levels,

---

* The Nazi death camp for women.

mutually impossible.
One the observable, external life,
everyday more horrible.
The other lived with God,
better every day,
truth upon truth,
glory upon glory.
The little Bible
I slipped from its worn sack
with hands that shook
seemed so mysterious,
all new to me,
as though it had been just written.
Sometimes I marveled that
the ink was dry.
I had believed the Bible always,
but now it had nothing to do with belief.
It was just a description of
the way things were—
of heaven and hell,
how people behave and how God acts.

Corrie Ten Boom, *Holland*

Women Who Light Lives

Seven women
sing the Chanukah blessings
the seventh night,
light two menorahs
each one candle on each.

Speaking out by turns
each of the seven women
describes and praises
a woman mentor
from her past
while the candles drip
onto a little tray.

Suddenly
we are fourteen women
in a double circle,
spirits connected
by stories we tell
or stories told about us,
witnesses
to the great miracle
of remembrance.

Joanne Seltzer

Purnima

before the first word
of the day

before I break my fast
and break my silence

before opening myself to traffic
before losing touch with sleep

hearing only the crowds of birds
hearing only a far-off voice in a temple chanting

seeing mists dissolve quickly in sun
seeing the newborn mountains

before losing touch with silence
while still touching sleep
before I forget to remember

let me sit down and recall
my blessings

Judy Kroll

We see you, see ourselves and know
That we must take the utmost care
And kindness in all things.

                              Joy Harjo

———————

How can you go on sleeping
when all of us are awake?
Wake up! Speak now and join us, hear our song!
                    Andal, *India, eighth century*
                    Translated by Jane Hirshfield

———————

Breakdown

I was terrified I'd break down.
I did.
It didn't matter.

                    Rosalind M. Baker, *England*

———————

I Taught Myself to Live Simply

I taught myself
to live simply and wisely

To look at the sky
and pray to God
and to wander long
before evening
to tire my
superfluous worries.

Anna Akhmatova,
Russia, 1889–1966

———————————

God Alone Suffices

Let nothing disturb you,
Let nothing dismay you.
All things pass
God never changes.
Patience attains
all that it strives for.
Those who have God
find they lack nothing.
God alone suffices.

Teresa of Avila,
Spain, 1515–82

May the Blessing of Rain Be on You

May the blessing of rain be on you,
the soft sweet rain.
May it fall upon your spirit
so that small flowers may spring up
and shed their sweetness in the air.

May the blessing of the great rains be on you
to beat upon your spirit and wash it clean;
and leave there many a shining pool
where the blue of heaven shines,
and sometimes a star.

May the blessing of the earth be on you,
the great round earth;
may you ever have a kindly greeting for people
as you're going along the roads.

And now may the Lord bless you,
and bless you kindly.
Amen

Celtic oral tradition,
Wales, England, Ireland, and Scotland

CHAPTER 4

Finding Heaven in Mother Earth

✳

A vein of sapphires
hides in the earth,
a sweetness in fruit;

and in plain-looking rock
lies a golden ore,
and in seeds,
the treasure of oil.

Like these,
the Infinite
rests concealed in the heart.

No one can see the ways
of our jasmine-white Lord.

Mahadevi, *India, twelfth century*
Translated by Jane Hirshfield

Sow in me your living breath,
As you sow a seed in the earth.

Kadya Molodowsky,
Russia, 1894–1975

His Heart Shone Right Out of His Eyes

As her own mother tells it, and she would know, Apijigo was cooking up a fine pot of stew when a deer approached, stood by the edge of her camp. Just waiting. Apijigo thought, Should I eat him or should I share with him? Which? She picked up her killing hatchet but when she finally advanced toward the deer and looked him in the eye, she felt ashamed. She knew hunger when she saw it. Just walked past the deer and chopped a little more wood for the fire. Finished that stew.

She put the stew onto the plate, set the plate down in front of the deer, got her own plate full, and ate sitting before him. He never moved. She ate the whole stew, mopped up every trace of it with bannock, pikwayzhigun, then sat quietly looking at him, crescent of horns, waiting. Unafraid. She had this feeling. Full. So this was what other people felt. She looked over at the deer. His eyes were steady and warm with a deep black light. His heart shone right out of his eyes.

He loves me, she thought. He loves me and I love him back.

Louise Erdrich

Play in this universe. Tend
All these shining things around you:
The smallest plant, the creatures and
objects in your care.
Be gentle and nurture. Listen ...

From a poem by
Anne Hillman

The Seven Directions

(STAND ON MOTHER EARTH. FACE EAST.)
Oh Great Spirit of the East, I face you to understand birth and new
beginnings. I look to you bringing forth a new day and am
reminded that life is about birth—of babies, puppies, new
seasons, new ways of doing things. Teach me the mysteries of
Beginnings.

(FACE SOUTH.)
Oh, Great Spirit of the South, I look to you to understand
abundance, fertility, warmth, and the extravagance and colors of
creation. Come to my mind and feet and lead me into the
adventures of the South.

(FACE WEST.)

Oh Spirit of the West, I turn to you to understand dying. As the sun goes down each day, I am reminded of many deaths: friends, generations, the seasons, and old ways of doing things. Let the sunset remind me that, like the sun, I too shall arise in a new life and color.

(FACE NORTH.)

Oh Strong, Powerful North, I face you to remember that life sometimes comes to us in cold and harshness. Not only do the days grow cold, but others may turn cold toward us. Give me the strength of the Buffalo, that I may stand in blizzards with my face toward the North, without being blown down or overwhelmed.

(FACE EAST AGAIN. LOOK UP.)

Oh Great Spirit of all that is *Up*, all that soars, all that floats or flies above us, all that comes to us from on high to enlighten us, I cherish this direction. Give me visions, and let my mind walk among the stars and moon, and in the daylight of the sun. Oh, sweet power of *Up*, lift me high to my Father, the Sky.

(STILL FACING EAST, LOOK DOWN.)

Oh Great Spirit of all that is *Down*, I thank you for my Mother, the Earth. I ask to be humble, to be simple, to never consider myself above all my relatives in creation. And may I walk with such respect upon the earth, that when it is time for me to go to her, she may receive me sweetly to her heart.

(STILL FACING EAST.)

Oh Wondrous Direction of *In,* I put my hand on my heart to remind me of the mysteries, the unknowns that lie within me. Teach me to guard the simpler beauties. To walk closely within the circle of my God in my heart. Let me share only with those who can be loyal to my secrets.

Ho! So it is!*

Iroquois oral tradition, Native American
Recorded by José Hobday

———————

The little cares that fretted me.
I lost them yesterday
Among the fields above the sea.
Among the winds at play;
Among the lowing of the herds,
The rustling of the trees,
Among the singing of the birds,
The humming of the bees.

———————

* The content of this prayer will vary every day and with every person. Only the form is given.

The foolish fears of what may happen,
I cast them all away
Among the clover-scented grass,
Among the new-mown hay;
Among the husking of the corn
Where drowsy poppies nod,
Where ill thoughts die and good are born,
Out in the fields with God.

Elisabeth Barrett Browning
England, 1806–61

Earth Teach Me

Earth teach me stillness
as the grasses are stilled with light.
Earth teach me suffering
as old stones suffer with memory.
Earth teach me humility
as blossoms are humble with beginning.
Earth teach me caring
as the mother who secures her young.

Nancy Wood

[T]he Holy may speak to you
from its
many hidden places
at any time.

The world
may whisper in your ear.

Or the spark of God in you
may whisper in your heart.

My grandfather showed me how
to listen.

Rachel Naomi Remen

The Sapphire

How can I focus my flickering, perceive
at the fountain's heart
the sapphire I know is there?

Denise Levertov,
England, 1923–98

How Should I Fear to Die?

How should I fear to die?
Have I not seen
The color of a small butterfly,
The silver sheen
Of breaking waves and a wood-dove's wings?
Have I not marked the coat
Of mouse and deer,
The shape of flowers, the thrush's speckled throat—
And shall I fear
To fall into the hands that made these things?

Teresa Hooley

The Stars

Stars on fire that populate night's far sky,
mute stars revolving blind, forever glazed,
you yank yesterdays out of our hearts
and throw us on tomorrows without consent.
We cry to you but all our cries are in vain.

We follow you since we must, arms linked,
eyes lifted to your pure but bitter light.

From your viewpoint all our suffering means little.
And so silent we stagger on—until suddenly
your divine fire is here in our hearts.

Simone Weil, *France, 1909–43*
Translated by Janine Canan

The mountain,
     I am part of it...
The herbs, the fir tree,
     I am part of it.
The morning mists, the clouds, the gathering waters,
     I am part of it.
The wilderness, the dew drops, the pollen...
     I am part of it.

Navajo, traditional chant

The Sacred Berry

(HOLD A RIPE STRAWBERRY, GREEN STEM INTACT.)
Oh sweet gift to the Seneca, I admire you. You are shaped like the heart
   to remind us that we are to live by the heart.
Your flesh is red, to tell us our hearts should be moist with blood,
   never dry and brown and crackly.

We study the seeds on the outside. They are many, to teach us that
    there are many ways in the world to believe, to understand life.
    All are worthy of respect.
We finger the leaves, so we keep in mind that we must always stay
    connected to Mother Earth and appreciate her gifts.
Now, we eat this beautiful strawberry from the bottom up (in silence),
    relishing the sweet taste. For the last bite we eat berry and leaf
    together to help us remember life holds bitter tastes with sweet. For
    all, we keep a thankful heart.

Seneca oral tradition, Native American,
recorded by José Hobday

This Island, This Season

The corn stalks are broken.
Potatoes are cached in dark corners,
onions and garlic braided
and hung. Gold peaches
in glass and plums'
rich ruby. Black pulp of berries
thickens in jars. Split cedar
is stacked by the door
and the lamps filled.

Anchored all night in the eyes
of this wind, the house
billows toward stars.

Alicia Hokanson

I know I am made from this earth, as my mother's hands were made
from this earth, as her dreams were made from this earth, and this
paper, these hands, this tongue speaking, all that I know speaks to me
through this earth and I long to tell you, you who are earth, too, and
listen as we speak to each other of what we know; the light is in us.

Susan Griffin

Spiritual Life

There is
no creation
that does not have a radiance,

Hildegard of Bingen,
Germany, 1098–1179

I think everything and everyone slept that afternoon in Little Rock. I sat with my dog in a cool place on the north side of my grandparent's clapboard home. Hydrangeas flourished there, shaded from the heat. The domed blue flowers were higher than our heads. I held the dog's head, stroking her into sleep. But she held my gaze. As I looked into her eyes I realized that I would never travel further than this into this animal's eyes. At this particular moment I was allowed to see infinity through my dog's eyes, and I was old enough to know that. They were as deep, as bewildering, as unattainable as a night sky. Just as mysterious was a clear awareness of water within me, the sound in my ears, yet resounding from my breast. It was a rumbling, rushing sound, the sound of moving water, waterfall water, white water. And I understood that these two things went together—the depth of a dark infinity and this energy of water. I understood, "This is who God is. My Mother is water and she is inside me and I am in the water."

Meinrad Craighead, *England*

How shall I begin my song
In the blue night that is settling?

Owl Woman, *mid-nineteenth
to early-twentieth century,
Papago people, Native American*

[72]

Earth is crammed with heaven,
and every common bush afire with God,
but only he who sees
takes off his shoes.

Elizabeth Barrett Browning,
England, 1806–61

The Prayer of the Cat

Lord,
I am the cat.
It is not, precisely, that I want something from You!
No.
I never ask for anything.
But
Should You have, by any chance,
in some heavenly barn
a little white mouse
or a saucer of milk,
I know of someone who would delight in them;
Or perhaps You might like someday
To place a curse on the whole race of dogs.

I would surely then say,
Amen.

Carmen Bernos de Gasztold,
France, c.1925–?

———————

My Lord,
Lord of the mountain grove,
At dawn
Hosts of warbling sparrows
Sing a song.
They keep repeating
Your name.

Andal, *India, eighth century*

———————

and how could anyone believe
that anything in this world
is only what it appears to be—

Mary Oliver

CHAPTER 5

For All Our Needs

❇

*Ti Prego**

This season, Lord,
I feel like the dogwood tree,
Twisted, wind-whipped,
    Frost-stripped,
Because the thaw came too quickly, Lord,
Too early—
Then the freeze.
The blooms hurt, Lord.
Trying to bud again
With tips ice-burnt,
Brown-burnt
Trying to feel spring, Lord,
Trying to feel, Lord,
Wanting to feel the bloom again,
        But when?

---

* *Ti prego* in Italian is the equivalent of "I plead with you," or "I pray you."

When, Lord, when?
    Amen

                                M. P. A. Sheaffer

God our Mother,
Living Water,
River of Mercy,
Source of Life,
in whom we live
and move
and have our being,
who quenches our thirst,
refreshes our weariness,
bathes
and washes
and cleanses
our wounds,
be for us always
a fountain of life,
and for all the world
a river of hope
springing up in the midst
of the deserts of despair.
Honor and blessing,

glory and praise
to You forever.

Amen.

Medical Mission Sisters

A Prayer for Spiritual Teachers

Jesus, please bless our spiritual teachers
Give them strength to nurture their fold
Help them to know by your example that they can
Be more than public saviors with private sins
Grant them the integrity to face their shadow side
And the willingness to explore and expose it
And the courage to reject its seduction
So that our spiritual teachers may set an example
For us to seek support, comfort and honesty
In all our relationships.

Nancy Steinbeck

Brigid's Feast

I should like a great lake of finest ale
for the King of kings.
I should like a table of the choicest food
for the family of heaven.
Let the ale be made from the fruits of faith
and the food be forgiving love.

I should welcome the poor to my feast,
for they are God's children.
I should welcome the sick to my feast,
for they are God's joy.
Let the poor sit with Jesus at the highest place,
and the sick dance with the angels.

God bless the poor,
God bless the sick,
and bless our human race.
God bless our food,
God bless our drink;
all homes, O God, embrace.

Brigid of Kildare Abbey,
Ireland, c.450–523

Give Me Someone

Lord,
When I am famished,
   Give me someone who needs food;
When I am thirsty,
   Send me someone who needs water;
When I am cold,
   Send me someone to warm;
When I am hurting,
   Send me someone to console; . . .
When I am poor,
   Lead someone needy to me;
When I have no time,
   Give me someone to help for a moment;
When I am criticized,
   Give me someone to praise;
When I am discouraged,
   Send me someone to encourage;
When I need another's understanding,
   Give me someone who needs mine;
When I need somebody to take care of me,
   Send me someone to care for;

When I think too much of myself,
  Turn my thoughts toward someone else.

Anonymous, twentieth century, Japan
Adapted from the translation of Mary-Theresa McCarthy

Different Ways to Pray

There were those who didn't care about praying.
The young ones. The ones who had
  been to America.
They told the old ones, *you are wasting your time.*
  Time? The old ones prayed for the young ones.
They prayed for Allah to mend their brains,
for the twig, the round moon,
to speak suddenly in a commanding tone.

From a poem by
Naomi Shihab Nye

May I be free from danger,
May I be free from fear,
May I be healthy,
May I dwell in peace.

May you be free from danger,
May you be free from fear,
May you be healthy,
May you dwell in peace.

May all beings be free from danger,
May all beings be free from fear,
May all beings be healthy,
May all beings dwell in peace.

Traditional Buddhist Prayer

———————————

Open our eyes to see our own part
in discord and aggression between people now;
forgive us our price and divisions,
and renew in us the search for peace,
so that trust may replace suspicion,
friendship replace fear.

From a prayer by
Angela Ashwin, *England*

Help in Old Age from the Mother
(after Psalm 71)

In you, Great Mother, I take refuge;
may I never be ashamed.

Be my refuge and my rock
where I may always dwell.

Keep me from the cruelties of age,
that I may never be alone.

You are my hope, Great Mother,
and have been since I was young.

In fact you were with me
in my mother's womb.

I thank you for my very life;
everyone knows I worship you.

Everyone knows you are my rock
and they hear me sing your praise.

Please don't forsake me in old age,
when my strength is almost gone.

I'm afraid I'll be mistreated,
sent away from the home I love.

I haven't lost my love for you,
I tell everyone about your power.

I tell everyone about your beauty;
I tell the world about your love.

You have taught me from childhood,
and still I learn from you every day.

Even in old age, wrinkled and gray-haired,
I am still your disciple.

I want to live to see
the return of the Mother to this earth.

Barbara Gibson

Make us ready, Lord,
    to serve others throughout the world
        who live and die
            in poverty and hunger.
Give them, through our hands, this day their daily bread,
and through our understanding love,
        give peace and joy.

Adapted from a prayer of
Mother Teresa of Calcutta,
Albania, 1910–97

Prayer for Village Earth
(for seven generations)

O Mother Earth, we pray today to link our spirits with all
our brothers and sisters who share this web of life with us
and to honor those who once walked upon this land.

Rest quiet, Ancient Ones, we seek only to honor you and
to respect the land. We will not take from it lightly, nor
do harm. We will respect those creatures with whom we
share this sacred place.

Eagle, Snake, Coyote and Lizard, we honor you! Bless us,
please you Flying People, Crawling People, the Swimmers,
Plants and Tree People, and all our four-legged brothers and
 sisters!

Father Sun, we beseech you to shine down your love
and light upon us!

Sister Rain and Brother Wind, walk softly here, for we are small
beneath your mighty power!

Sister Moon, shine gently as you guide us into dreamtime, and
when you journey across the world, send your stars to light
our way home!

O Mother Earth, accept our prayer, bless us with your energy
and healing. Help us to remember that we are connected to all
who share your sacred web of life . . . past, present, and future,
that in divinity and grace, we may exist as one!

Sharon Auberle

Prayer for Beauty

Watch over us,
Your hand before us, protect us,
Heal us, make us well.
As you speak to us, we speak to you:
    May it be beautiful before us.
    May it be beautiful behind us.
    May it be beautiful below us.
    May it be beautiful above us.
    May it be beautiful everywhere.
    Restore us in beauty.
    Restore us in beauty.

Changing Woman, *Navajo,*
Native American

Prayer for a Child
While Listening to Rachmaninoff

Bless this child, whose blue eyes widen
as the notes swell and bless the wonder
of their new-soul depths.
Bless this sun-glazed evening and the green chair
where I rock her to sleep, adrift in music and light.

Bless the touch of her tiny hand as my eyes
grow heavy and hers close, sailing off
into that orange sky of sleep.
Bless the genius of her miniature thumb,
surpassing the wonder of Rachmaninoff and sunset,
and bless the grace that shows me
somewhere lives a smiling God.

Sharon Auberle

———————————

Prayer for Wellness

Oh Great Spirit—
   Grandfather—
      Grandmother—

Help us with the power
of the Thunder-Beings
To admit the pain that has
led us to shut out your Wisdom.

Open our memories to the
lives of our Ancestors
To the ways of relating
in Traditional Harmony.

Shine the light of New Days
on our lives
To open our eyes to what
we cannot see in the
darkness of Dysfunction.

Tie us to all the Peoples
who walk this Sacred Path
To the Spirit within us,
our source of life and support.

Oh Great Spirit—
    Grandfather—
        Grandmother—

Help us to accept our history that we may be wise.
Help us to use our memories to revive our ways.
Help us to use our vision to see new paths clearly.
Help us to accept our spirits to be our strength.

To stand with feet firmly planted on this good Earth.
To speak only that which comes from the Truth.
To be Proud.
To HEAL WITH DIGNITY.

Maria Cristina Gonzalez

Metta Prayer

May I be well, loving, and peaceful.
May I be at ease in my body, feeling the ground beneath my feet and
    letting my back be long and straight, enjoying breath as it rises and
    falls and rises.
May I know and be intimate with body mind, whatever its feeling or
    mood,
    calm or agitated, tired or energetic, irritated or friendly.
Breathing in and out, in and out, aware, moment by moment,
    of the risings and passings.
May I be attentive and gentle towards my own discomfort and
    suffering.
May I be attentive and grateful for my own joy and well-being.
May I move towards others freely and with openness.
May I receive others with sympathy and understanding.
May I move towards the suffering of others with peaceful and attentive
    confidence.
May I recall the Boddhisattva of compassion;
    her 1000 hands, her instant readiness for action.
    Each hand with an eye in it, the instinctive knowing what to do.
May I continually cultivate the ground of peace for myself and others
    and persist, mindful and dedicated to this work, independent of
    results.

May I know that my peace and the world's peace are not separate;
   that our peace in the world is a result of our work for justice.
May all beings be well, happy, and peaceful.

                                                        Maylie Scott

——————————————

CHAPTER 6

At Work

❀

A Zen Prayer for Preparing a Meal:
How To Stuff a Pepper

Take your green pepper, and gently,
for peppers are shy. No matter which side
you approach, it's always the back side.
Perched on green buttocks, the pepper sleeps.
In its silk tights, it dreams
of somersaults and parsley,
of the days when the sexes were one.

Slash open the sleeve
as if you were cutting a paper lantern,
and enter a moon, spilled like a melon,
a fever of pearls,
a conversation of glaciers.
It is a temple built to the worship
of morning light.

I have sat under the great globe
of seeds on the roof of that chamber,
too dazzled to gather the taste I came for.
I have taken the pepper in hand,
smooth and blind, a runt in the rich
evolution or roses and ferns.
You say I have not yet taught you
to stuff a pepper?
Cooking takes time.

Next time we'll consider the rice.

Nancy Willard

Kalighat*

Bhogobaan ekane ache,
Mother Teresa whispered in Bengali
as she went from bed to bed:
God is here.

---

* *Mother Teresa's home for the dying destitute in Calcutta, Kalighat was reputedly the hardest assignment in her worldwide community. Anita Mathias is a former member of the community.*

Her creased face looked sweet and sad.
"This is *Bhogobaan ki badi*,
God's house,"
the sisters told new arrivals,
believing that Kalighat is sanctified
in its very stones
by the thousands who have died
peaceful deaths here.

Perhaps the light created this aura.
The light spilled from high windows
through a filigreed lattice,
spilled into the dim room
with a stippled radiance
that made working there
an epiphany.

Anita Mathias

You Can Also Pray While You Work

You can also pray while you work. Work doesn't stop prayer. And prayer doesn't stop work. It requires only that small raising of the mind to God. "I love you, God. I trust you. I believe in you. I need you now." Small things like that. They are wonderful prayers.

Mother Teresa of Calcutta, *Albania, 1910–97*

A Pediatrician's Prayer for Perfection

See how she grabs my finger?
Your daughter is strong, what a grasp!
Look how she roots around for the nipple
When I stroke her cheek.
(*Let this baby be as perfect inside as outside.*
May her heart murmur be as innocent as she is.
Let her not stop breathing one morning for no reason, and,
When her mother picks her up from an extra-long nap,
Be already cold to the touch.)
Perfectly normal, that's perfectly normal!
Oh, she only has eyes for her mother, see,
She's looking at you!
(*Now that this baby girl is delivered, deliver her from infection,*
Structural defects, neoplasm, metabolic deficiencies, and

From shaking by the boyfriend who is not her father,
From smothering by her mother who needs mothering herself.)
Your daughter is perfect, absolutely perfect!
(More than anything,
Let me not have made a mistake.)

Jan Steckel, M.D.

What Must I Do?

God know my situation.
I am but one,
but I am one.
I cannot do everything,
but I can do something.

Bishop Barbara Clementine Harris

Litany of Sorrow for Denying Women Authority

MEN AND WOMEN SAY:
We have denied the authority of women
And limited our gifts;

WOMEN:
But "nothing is veiled that will not be revealed."
"Nothing is hidden that will not be made known."

MEN:
We have feared those who are not like us.
We have refused to show our weakness.
We have locked away part of ourselves.

MEN AND WOMEN:
But "nothing is veiled that will not be revealed."
"Nothing is hidden that will not be made known."

WOMEN:
We have feared those who are like us;
We have refused to know our strength.
We have locked away part of ourselves.

Men and Women:
But "nothing is veiled that will not be revealed."
"Nothing is hidden that will not be made known."

Men:
We have resisted the Wisdom of God
And not sought Her face.

Women:
We have turned aside from Her image
And hidden our knowledge of Her.

Men and Women:
But have no fear.
For "nothing is veiled that will not be revealed."
"Nothing is hidden that will not be made known."

*Adapted from a prayer for the first ordination of
Anglican women, London, March 31, 1987*

Litany of Blessing for a Woman Taking Authority

Women say:
Blessed is she who believed there would be a fulfillment of what was
   spoken to her by the Lord.

WOMEN AND MEN:
Blessed are you among women.

MEN:
May you speak with the voice of the voiceless, and give courage to
those in despair.

WOMEN:
May you feed the hungry of mind and heart,
And send away satisfied those who are empty.

MEN:
May you be strong to confront injustice, and powerful to rebuke the
arrogant.

WOMEN:
May you not be alone but find support in your struggle and sisters to
rejoice with you.

MEN:
May your vision be fulfilled in company with us; may you have
brothers on your journey.

WOMEN:
Blessed is she who believed there would be a fulfillment of what was
    spoken to her by the Lord.

WOMEN AND MEN:
Blessed are you . . .

*Adapted from a prayer for the first
ordination of Anglican women,
London, March 31, 1987*

———————

I saw God in an instant of time,
in my understanding,
and by this vision
I saw that God is present in all things . . .
And God said to me:
I thank you
for your service and your labor,
and especially in your youth.

Julian of Norwich, *England, 1342–c.1423*

My Poems

come to me hard fisted
with mean mouths
they are not polite ladies
will not be still
they won't stay where I put them
nor keep my secrets.
I like their red rough hands,
their ready grins
the way they yank and unravel
my bindings, and won't let me sleep
until they let loose my soul.

Nita Penfold

Prayer Before Work

Great one, austere
By whose intent the distant star
Holds its course clear,
Now make this spirit soar—
Give it that ease.

From a poem by
May Sarton

Lord of all the world, in your hand is all blessing. I come now to revere your holiness by baking bread, and I ask you to bless all the ingredients. Send an angel to watch over my baking, so that all will be done well, the bread will rise perfectly, and will not be burned. These baked goods will honor the holy Sabbath when holy blessings will be recited. Bless my work as you blessed the dough of Sarah and Rebecca, our mothers. My Lord God, listen to my voice, for you are the God who hears the voices of those who call upon you wholeheartedly. May you be praised to eternity.

Adapted from a traditional Jewish prayer

Cleaning Rice

On the balcony of my courtyard I sit
Cleaning rice, picking out the tiny black pebbles.
On the wings of a warm breeze
The music of my neighbor rises to my ear.
His musical arrangements, like sweet scent,
Intangibly sink into my being.
The music stops.
He leaves, the courtyard gate closes behind him.
"Alla Aqbar," chants the muezzin in the mosque on the Mount.
It is noon.
Loudspeakers throughout the walled City

Transmit his call.
And I sit, in my high-walled courtyard,
Cleaning the rice.

Ruth Fogelman, *Israel*

Too Much to Do

How is it, my God, that you have given me this hectic life and so little time to enjoy your presence. All day, people are waiting to speak to me, and even during meals I have to keep talking to people about their concerns and needs. During sleep itself I am still thinking and dreaming about the problems that wait for me tomorrow. I am doing all this for you, not for myself. My way of life is more tormenting than reward, and I only hope that for you it is a gift of love. I know you are always beside me, yet I become so busy that I forget you and ignore you. If you want me to keep up this pace, please make me think about you and love you, even during the most hectic activity. If you do not want me to be so busy, please release me from it and teach me how others can take over some of my responsibilities.

Teresa of Avila, *Spain, 1515–82*

Radiating Pain

Doctor,
what I want
is to feel the same.
I want
to curl up in an overstuffed chair with a good book
to settle down casually next to someone and strike up a conversation
to sit on a park bench and eat my lunch
to buy a week's worth of groceries and carry them all upstairs at once
to run along a trail next to the water
to wear shoes that aren't sneakers or Birkenstocks
to drive my fire-engine red Ford Galaxy from Mexico to Oregon again
to ride my motorbike down slippery mud ravines
to dance at the wedding instead of standing in the back of the church
to sit through the bar mitzvah instead of lurking in synagogue shadows
to accept the folding white lawn chair thoughtfully provided at the
    graveside
to lift up the girl-child who is asking to sit on my lap
to sit astride my man while making love
to have him come up behind me and put his hand on my shoulder
    without every muscle in my back clenching
to lean back when he kisses me and not feel that tightness grabbing at
    me
and almost see the line of fire shooting down my leg

or just lie alone in my bed at night and not be aware
that my left leg feels any different from the right
or that I am any different from anyone else
who takes these things for granted.

Jan Steckel, M.D.

———————

May there always be work for your hands to do
May your purse always hold a coin or two
May the sun always shine through your window pane
May a rainbow be certain to follow each rain
May the hand of a friend be near to you
May God fill your heart to gladden you.

Anonymous, ancient Ireland

———————

Doing the Best We Can

When we do the best we can,
We never know what miracles await.

Helen Keller, *1880–1968*

The Great Work

Lord, in the presence of your love, I ask that you unite my work with your great work, and bring it to fulfillment. Just as a drop of water, poured into a river, becomes one with the flowing waters, so may all I do become part of all that you do. So that those with whom I live and work may also be drawn to your love.

Gertrude of Helfta, *Germany 1256–c.1302*

Go Forward Securely

What you hold, may you always hold. What you do, may you always do, and never abandon. But with swift pace, light step, and unswerving feet, go forward securely, joyfully, and lightly, on wisdom's path. Believing nothing, agreeing with nothing, which would dissuade you from your resolution. Or which would place a stumbling block for you on the way. So that you may offer your promises to the Most High God, in the pursuit of the sacred goals to which the Spirit has summoned you.

Clare of Assisi, *Italy, 1194–1253*

CHAPTER 7

Grateful for *Everything*

❀

Magnificat

My soul magnifies God
Luke 1:46

What shall I do
with this quiet joy?
It calls forth the expanse
of my soul, calls
it forth to go singing
through the world,
calls it forth
to rock the cradles of death
   gently
and without fear,
to collect the rain
in my hands
and spill it
   like laughter,

calls it forth
to touch and carry
her suffering, his age
our dense flesh,

     to bear into this world
a place
where light will glisten
the edge of every wing
and blade of grass,
shine along every hair on every head,
gleam among the turnings of every wave,
glorify
   the turning open of each life,
each human hand.

                        Christina Hutchins

Unexpected Blessings

Give thanks
For unknown blessings
Already on their way.

           Anonymous Native American prayer

To Sing Is to Praise

To sing is to love and to affirm, to fly and soar, to coast into the hearts of the people who listen, to tell them that life is to live, that love is there, that nothing is a promise, but that beauty exists, and must be hunted for and found. That death is a luxury, better to be romanticized and sung about than dwelt upon in the face of life. To sing is to praise God and the daffodils, and to praise God is to thank Him, in every note within my small range, and every color in the tones of my voice, with every look into the eyes of my audience, to thank Him. Thank you, God, for letting me be born, for giving me eyes to see the daffodils lean in the wind, all my brothers, all my sisters, for giving me ears to hear crying, legs to come running, hands to smooth damp hair, a voice to laugh with and to sing with . . . to sing to you and the daffodils . . . which are you.

Joan Baez

Faithfulness

May you be blessed forever, Lord, for not abandoning me
    when I abandoned you.
May you be blessed forever, Lord, for offering your hand of love
    in my darkest, most lonely moment.
May you be blessed forever, Lord, for putting up with such
    A stubborn soul as mine.

May you be blessed forever, Lord, for loving me
more than I love myself.
May you be blessed forever, Lord, for continuing to pour out your
blessings upon me, even though I respond so poorly.
May you be blessed forever, Lord, for drawing out the goodness in
people, including me.
May you be blessed forever, Lord, for repaying our sins with
your love.
May you be blessed forever, Lord, for being constant and unchanging,
amidst all the changes in the world.
May you be blessed forever, Lord, for your countless blessings on me
and on every creature in the world.

Teresa of Avila, *Spain, 1515–82*

————————

For the Darkness

For the darkness of waiting
Of not knowing what is to come
Of staying ready and quiet and attentive,
We praise you, o God.

For the darkness and the light
Are both alike to you.

For the darkness of staying silent
For the terror of having nothing to say
And for the greater terror
Of needing to say nothing,
We praise you, o God.

For the darkness and the light
Are both alike to you.

For the darkness of loving
In which it is safe to surrender
To let go of our self-protection
And to stop holding back our desire,
We praise you, o God.

For the darkness and the light
Are both alike to you.

For the darkness of choosing
when you give us the moment
to speak, and act, and change,
and we cannot know what we have set in motion,
but we still have to take the risk,
We praise you, o God.

For the darkness and the light
Are both alike to you.

For the darkness of hoping
In a world which longs for you,
For the wrestling and the laboring of all creation
For wholeness and justice and freedom,
We praise you, o God.

For the darkness and the light
Are both alike to you.

Adapted from an Anglican Litany
prayed in Canterbury Cathedral,
April 18, 1986

To Our First Grandmother

We are thankful to our first Grandmother, the Moon, who lights the nighttime sky. She is our leader. She watches over the ocean's tides. By her face we measure the passing of the days. She watches over us when a child arrives. We send greetings and thanks to Grandmother Moon.

Mohawk oral tradition, Native American

Gratitude

Gratitude for the trees
That shared their bodies
For this book

Gratitude for the many friends
Along the way

Gratitude to time and space
Within which to be creative

Gratitude for
Above and Below
Inside and All Around
For inspiration

Gratitude for the All
That is beyond any words
Mystery dwelling between the lines

And thank you to the Old One
That is ever being born.

—Amen

Rosemary Partridge

[113]

Celtic Thanksgiving

O gentle Christ, ever thanks to Thee,
That Thou from the dark has raised me free
And from the coldness of last night's space
To the gentle light of this day's grace.

Celtic oral tradition,
Wales, England, Ireland, and Scotland

All you clear and shimmering waters, . . .
All you tiny insects hovering over the water
All the winds in the trees
All you bass that avoid our lures
All you loons that glide and dive
All you chipmunks and squirrels and baby rabbits
that eat from our doorstep
All you huge rocks and palisades
All you silent canoes
All you early morning fishermen,
Praise the Lord.

From a poem by
Pat Corrick Hinton

Thank you, my dear,

You came, and you did
well to come: I needed
you. You have made

love blaze up in
my breast—bless you!
Bless you as often

as the hours have
been endless to me
while you were gone.

Mary Bernard

Theology

If the flies did not hurry themselves to the window
they'd still die somewhere.

Other creatures choose the other dimension:
                                        to slip
into a thicket, swim into the shaded, undercut
part of the stream.

My dog would make her tennis ball
disappear into just such a hollow,
pushing it under the water with both paws.
Then dig for it furiously, wildly, until it popped up again.

A game or a theology, I could not tell.

The flies might well prefer the dawn-ribboned mouth of a trout,
its crisp and speed,
                              if they could get there,
though they are not in truth that kind of fly
and preference is not given often in these matters.

A border collie's preference is to do anything entirely,
with the whole attention. This Simone Weil called prayer.
And almost always, her prayers were successful—
                                                              the tennis ball
could be summoned again to the surface.

When a friend's new pound dog, diagnosed distempered,
doctored for weeks, crawled under the porch to die, my friend crawled
     after,
pulled her out, said "No!,"

as if to live were just a simple matter of training.
                                The coy-dog, startled, obeyed.
Now trots out to greet my car when I come to visit.

Only a firefly's evening blinking outside the window,
this miraculous story, but everyone hurries to believe it.

                                        Jane Hirshfield

————————————

Thank You

Listen
With the night falling we are saying thank you...

with the animals dying around us
our lost feelings we are saying thank you
in the forests falling faster than the minutes
of our lives we are saying thank you
with the words going out like cells of a brain
with the cities growing over us like the earth faster and faster
we are saying thank you
with nobody listening we are saying thank you
we are saying thank you and waving
dark though it is.

                                From a poem by Anne Lamott

I Arise Today

I arise today
Through a mighty strength:
   God's power to guide me,
   God's might to uphold me,
   God's wisdom to teach me,
   God's eyes to watch over me,
   God's ear to hear me,
   God's word to give me speech,
   God's hand to guard me,
   God's way to lie before me,
   God's shield to shelter me,
   God's host to secure me.

Brigid of Kildare Abbey,
Ireland, c.450–523

The Flowers

The flowers come and go
Filled with light
Breath and color
Reminders
That some things
Can be counted on
To bud and bloom
Linger awhile
Then die
The meaning of their life is
    known
By the hands that held them
The bowl that contained them
The hearts that loved them
The air that was filled
With their fragrance
And
The breath-taking change
They made in the Universe
Wherever they were

Betty McAfee

Praise to You Spirit of Fire!

Praise to you
Spirit of Fire!
To you who sound the timbrel
And the lyre.

Your music sets our minds
Ablaze! The strength of our souls
Awaits your coming.

There the mounting will
Gives the soul its savor
And desire is its lantern.

Insight invokes you in a cry
Full of sweetness, while reason
Builds you temples as she labors
At her golden crafts.

Hildegard of Bingen,
Germany, 1098–1179

Give Thanks for Everything

Give thanks for everything you have,
For everything you receive,
And for everything you are going to receive.
Never cease to give thanks,
For this positive attitude towards life—
The very act of giving thanks—
Draws the best out of you,
Helps to keep your heart and mind open;
Helps to keep your awareness expanding.
The more blessings you count,
The more they increase.

Adapted from a poem by
Eileen Caddy

CHAPTER 8

Out of Darkness

Mother Wisdom Speaks

Some of you I will hollow out.
I will make you a cave.
I will carve you so deep the stars will shine in your darkness.
You will be a bowl.
You will be the cup in the rock collecting rain. . . .

I will do this because the world needs the hollownesss of you.
I will do this for the space that you will be.
I will do this because you must be large.
A passage.
People will find their way through you.
A bowl.
People will eat from you
and their hunger will not weaken them to death.
A cup to catch the sacred rain. . . .

Light will flow in your hollowing.
You will be filled with light.
Your bones will shine.
The round open center of you will be radiant.
I will call you Brilliant One.
I will call you Daughter Who is Wide.
I will call you transformed.

From a poem by
Christine Lore Webber

Why Do You Hide Yourself?

Why, O my Love, my Life, my Light, do you hide yourself from me?
Why does that heart which I have felt beat against my own a thousand
times, whose fiery heat has warmed my soul over and over again, why
is that very heart unconscious of my needs and hurt today, when yesterday we were one. Why is it that living as I do in the presence of
your burning love, everything near me today is as ice, indifference, and
pain? Why, Love of my loves, my heaven, my own, my all, why do you
leave my soul to drown in an ocean of loneliness?

Concepcion Cabrera de Armida (Conchita), *Mexico, 1862–1932*

Dear God, it is so hard for us not to be anxious,
we worry about work and money,
about food and health,
about weather and crops,
about war and politics,
about loving and being loved.
Show us how perfect love casts out fear.

Monica Furlong, *England*

Passing the Refugee Camp

Yesterday the soldiers smashed
Lena's sink and tub and tiles

They whipped a father in front of his sons
ages 2 and 4

They do this all the time
The house filled with water

They locked the door on the crying boys
taking the father

Believe me Lena says
They had no reason

On the steps of the National Palace Hotel
soldiers peel oranges

throwing back their heads so the juice
runs down their throats

This must be their coffee break
guns slung sideways

They are laughing
stripping lustily

They know what sweetness lives within
How can they know this and forget

so many other things?

From a poem by
Naomi Shihab Nye

For Victims of War and Refugees

O, God, you bring hope out of emptiness
energy out of fear
new life out of grief and loss;
comfort all who have lost their homes
through persecution, war, exile, or
deliberate destruction.
Give them security, a place to live,
and neighbors they trust
to be, with them,
a new sign of peace to the world.

Abridged from a poem by
Janet Morley, *England*

Lament for September 11, 2001
(after Psalm 137)

By the shores of the Hudson River,
we sat down and wept
when we remembered our city.

We have stopped singing
because Fear and Hate, our captors,

torment us with memories of the past,
saying, "You'll never sing like you used to."

How can we be joyful
in the midst of such devastation?

If we forget you, Manhattan,
if we forget the dead,
may our right hands wither.

Let our tongues stick to our mouths
if we forget those we have lost,
only to return to our proud and ignorant ways.

Remember, O Distant God,
the day of disaster in the city.

Defeat our captors,
Fear and Hate, who scream
"Tear down Afghanistan!
Tear it down to the foundations!"

O Fear and Hate, you devastate us!
You make us long for revenge,

you make us learn to bomb small villages.
You make us desire the suffering of others.

Remember, O Distant God,
the day of disaster in the city,
and save us from our proud and ignorant ways.

Barbara Gibson

The Next Day: 9/12/01

Bless the black Mercedes cutting me off
bless the cell phone and the ear

pressed against it. Bless the sneakers
running between shadows to the park,

the workers trying to save the diseased elm.
Bless the elm,

the suit jacket draped over an arm,
the bent arm, the shoulder covered

in oxford cloth, the neck and tie.
Bless the pulse in the neck.

Bless the high-heels rushing, the wheels
on the stroller, the cursing mouth.

the hand tossing the coffee cup,

Bless the pissing in the bushes,

the singing in the car.
the breath visible in cold air.

Bless how we forgot.

Ann-Marie Madden Irwin

———————————

For the 500th Dead Palestinian: Ibtisam Bozieh

LITTLE SISTER Ibtisam,
our sleep flounders, our sleep tugs
the cord of your name.
Dead at 13, for staring through
the window into a gun barrel
which did not know you wanted to be
a doctor.

From a poem by
Naomi Shihab Nye

In the Cemetery of Your City:
Israel, March 6, 2002

In the cemetery of your city
You grieve by the freshly filled grave
You deny that this is really happening—
Your child, your grandchild—
Lifeless.
Why are you standing there—alive
While your progeny lies under earth?
"Unreal, unreal," you say,
As tears well in your eyes
And drizzle down your cheek.
You stand, gazing at the name
Stuck on a small stick
Atop the freshly shoveled earth.
Is this all that is left of your dream?
Or is this just one bad dream
From which you will awaken?
Dazed, you lick the salty liquid from your lip.
A deep voice rises:
"*Yitgadal veyitkadash....*"
And you walk away to the hole in your home.

Ruth Fogelman, *Israel*

What Is Happening

Moment to moment
we ask, what is happening?
The sound of shattering everywhere,
is it the world, fragmenting at last,
or our own hearts cracking,
the final break-up of ice?

Dorothy Walters

Prayer from Auschwitz

You have made me so rich, oh God; please let me share out Your
beauty with open hands. My life has become an uninterrupted dialogue with You, oh God, one great dialogue. Sometimes when I stand
in some corner of the camp, my feet planted on Your earth, my eyes
raised toward Your Heaven, tears sometimes run down my face, tears
of deep emotion and gratitude. At night, too, when I lie in bed and rest
in You, oh God, tears of gratitude run down my face, and that is my
prayer.

Etty Hillesum, *Netherlands, d. 1943 in Auschwitz*
Translated by Otto Pomerans

Bodhi

Some days are like this,
you wake with an ache in your chest
that isn't even yours.
You know that somewhere, great rivers
    of blood are being shed.
Somewhere, mothers are weeping over
    children, bodies strewn like wildflowers.
Somewhere, men and women eat a bowl of pain—
A man tells his wife that he is leaving,
A woman wakes in an empty bed
or puts her hand to an empty place
    where a breast was.
Somewhere, in the screeching of brakes
    there is a shattering, of glass, of lives.
This earth is covered in a sea of suffering.
If for a few moments we manage to forget
    do not begrudge us our wine, our prayer, our reaching out
        for a word, a touch,

    even from a stranger.

Regina Sara Ryan

Troparion*

Lord,
This woman who encountered her shadow
    perceives the numinous in You,
    leads the women who come with grief
    and myrrh to Your grave.
Alas! What a desperate night I've traveled through:
    extravagant the desire, dark and moonless
    the need of a passionate body.
Accept this spring of tears,
    You who empty the seawater from the clouds.
Bend to the pain in my heart, You
    whose incarnation bent the sky
    and left it empty.
I will wash your feet with kisses,
    dry them with my hair, feet that Eve once heard
    at dusk in Paradise, then hid in fear.
You who are limitless mercy—who will trace the results
    of a lifetime I've done wrong, evaluate
    my weakness? I ask, remember me
    if nothing else, as one who lived.

Kassiane, c.804–?, Byzantium,
Translated by Liana Sakelliou

---

*an Eastern Orthodox hymn in the voice of Mary Magdalen

Not Without Longing

Come, rest
inside this house
you left
to travel so far. Home
now, you see
the sleeping mountain
was here all along—
the braided rope of the past
no longer someone else
you must look for. The heart
left open will heal itself
all over again
as the daring moon
slowly rises.

Karen Benke

In the morning the waking was slow
as the cool breeze blew in
from the open patio, and there
was no need for rush or hurry.

The sun cast a yellow hue
through the drapes and she sighed
wanting to continue the deep breathing
of the sleep she had craved.

She was alone now. By choice this time.
Only the birdsong greeted her
from the tree branch that brushed
against the bedroom window.

The sweet fragrance of the early breeze
filled her up with springtime.
For a long time she lay there
letting the morning embrace her.

With a deep yawn she moved
into consciousness.
She was not shaken
by this recent turn of events.
It was better this way.

From the warm cocoon of bed
into the kiss of the morning sun
she rose again.
And life was new.

Linda S. Boerstler

———————————

I saw you in the doorway.
You were black and bruised and broken.
I knew you were someone's daughter.

You are your mother's daughter.
If she could, she would sit with you
and say how much she loved you.

I saw you in the shelter.
You looked much older than your years.
Your kids were tired and making a fuss.
I knew you were someone's daughter.

You are your mother's daughter.
Imagine her here as a sister a friend,
saying how much she loves you.

I saw you on the news last night
on a dirt road in Soweto.
They were screaming at you.
You had no shoes.
I know you were someone's daughter.

You are your mother's daughter
and she is her mother's daughter.
She has put up with so much abuse.
That shows how much she loves you.

I saw you in the delivery room
in drug withdrawal, writhing.
They say you have AIDS. You are three hours old,
and I know you are someone's daughter.

You are your mother's daughter
and she needs you to forgive her.
She doesn't know how to love as yet,
but when she does, I promise you,
she will say how much she loves you.

I saw you in an orphanage.
How sad you looked, and lonely.

They say that you are hard to place,
but I know you are someone's daughter.

You are your mother's daughter
and a foster mother's daughter,
and one of these days, she will come for you
and say how much she loves you.

I saw you in a nursing home.
You were slumped in a chair with a vacant stare.
I knew you were somebody's daughter.

You are your mother's daughter,
your Mother God's own daughter.
Soon, very soon, She will come for you
and say how much She loves you.

Miriam Therese Winter

———————

From moment to moment
one can bear much.

Teresa of Avila,
Spain, 1515–82

May the angel of God make smooth the road,
May the angel of God be carrying you home.

Celtic oral tradition,
Wales, England, Ireland, and Scotland

Psalms of a Laywoman

I suffered, and now there is joy,
I was lonely, and now there is comfort,
I was desolate, and now there is warmth.
I was empty, and now there is fullness.

From a prayer by
Edwina Gately

There is a Brokenness

There is a brokenness
out of which comes the unbroken,
a shatteredness out
of which blooms the unshatterable.
There is a sorrow
beyond all grief which leads to joy
and a fragility
out of whose depths emerges strength.

There is a hollow space
too vast for words
through which we pass with each loss,
out of whose darkness
we are sanctioned into being.

There is a cry deeper than all sound
whose serrated edges cut the heart
as we break open
to the place inside which is unbreakable
and whole,
while learning to sing.

Rashani

CHAPTER 9

Our Spiritual and Mystical Experience

❋

Preparing to Greet the Goddess

Do not think of her
until you are prepared
to be driven to your limits,
to rush forth from yourself
like a ritual bowl overflowing
with consecrated wine.

Do not summon her image
unless you are ready to be blinded,
to stand in the flash
of a center exploding,
yourself shattering into the landscape,
wavering bits of bark and water.

Do not speak her name
until you have said goodbye
to all your familiar trinkets—

your mirrors, your bracelets,
your childhood adorations—
From now on you are nothing,
a ghost hovering at the window,
a voice singing under water.

Dorothy Walters

Fire in Water

I have been told,
"The sun on deep waves is beautiful."
And have dreamed on those words.
I will dive down to the edge of darkness,
to see where fire is drowned
in understanding.

Fiona Davidson

As a silkworm weaves
her home, with love,
from her own threads,
wrapping herself
round and round,
and dying becomes,

I burn
with the heart's desire.

O Lord, break into
my greed, and show
me your way through.

O White Jasmine Lord
                    Mahadevi, *India, twelfth century*

———————————

you

of the psalms
and the river
who fill up my pitcher
with water

you
of my breath
and my dream—
sleeper beside me
in bed
you—

[145]

cottonwood tree
in the early morning
the garbage truck rattles
its cans—

i wait by the well
all day
you don't come
all night

you
are seven time zones away
in a land known to sailors in homer
the e-mail is down
i can't reach

you
to whom mirabai spoke
you
who are covered with flowers
sent out to sea on a raft
you
to whom rilke is whispering
of terrible angels

you
whom i lost
when i entered this world
and learned to say

you
in words—

you
break into my night—
rattle my rib cage—
make biblical claims
                    on my flesh—

                    you
                    two A.M. terror
                    lusting for what
                            you have made—

lord of the apple tree—
angel with fangs—

i spit like an old jewish woman—
water to dust
in your hands—

suddenly everything's
    hot—

        fire
        on the mountain—

        you—

        burning
        in me—

        never
        consumed—

                Naomi Ruth Lowinsky

—————————————

The desert waits,
ready for those who come,
who follow the Spirit's leading
or are driven,
because they will not come any other way.

                Adapted from a poem by
                Ruth Burgess

Enter and penetrate,
O Spirit. Come and bless
This hour.

Madeleine L'Engle

The Sacredness of Time

Within the holy light that sweeps across the world, illumining all that is dark, warming all that is cold, the sacred cycle of time unfolds through the moon's great revolutions, the turning seasons and flowing tides, birds rushing south and returning north again. At the center of sacred time, the high purpose and meaning of all existence is revealed and concealed, a miracle and a mystery.

No words lie deep enough to explain or convey the holiness of time eternally cycling and spiraling through the vast universe. Sacred Scriptures hint at the Truth in sublime and simple images:

For everything there is a season
    And a time for every matter under heaven;
A time to be born, and a time to die;
    A time to plant, and a time to reap;
A time to harm, and a time to heal;
    A time to break down, and a time to build up;

A time to weep, and a time to laugh;
    A time to mourn, and a time to dance. (Ecclesiastes 3.1–5)

Within these unending cycles of change, of loss and newness that sacred time brings in its wake, each life unfolds in passages that bring to an end forever something that was and create something entirely new. Unplanned, unexpected, unpredictable—for the Spirit works through surprises—these transition times, these transformative years, weave each thread of experience into a pattern of shining completeness, fulfillment, peace. As a Holy Day imprints the bleak circle of a year with meaning, so great moments in every lifespan mark it indelibly with direction and Divinity.

Mary Ford-Grabowsky

Speak and Write What You See and Hear!

And behold! In the forty-third year of my earthly course, as I was
gazing with great fear and trembling attention at a heavenly vision,
I saw a blazing light in which resounded a voice from heaven, saying
    to me:
"O fragile human, dust to dust! Speak and write what you see and
    hear!
And since you are timid in speaking, and simple in expressing, and
    untaught

in writing, speak and write these things not by shallow human understanding,
and not by the rules and requirements of grammar, but as you see and
hear them
on high in the heavenly places, in the wonders of God."

                        Hildegard of Bingen, *Germany, 1098–1179*

Dangerous Prayers

Deliver us, O God, O Truth, O Love, from quiet prayer
from polite and politically correct language,
from appropriate gesture and form
and whatever else we think we must put forth to invoke
or to praise You.

Let us instead pray dangerously—
wantonly, lustily, passionately.
Let us demand with every ounce of our strength,
let us storm the gates of heaven, let us shake up ourselves
and our plaster saints from the sleep of years.

Let us pray dangerously.
Let us throw ourselves from the top of the tower,
let us risk a descent to the darkest region of the abyss,

let us put our head into the lion's mouth
and direct our feet to the entrance of the dragon's cave.

Let us pray dangerously.
Let us not hold back a little portion,
dealing out our lives—our precious minutes and our
energies—like some efficient accountant.
Let us rather pray dangerously—unsafe, profligate, wasteful!

Let us ask for nothing less than the Infinite to ravage us.
Let us ask for nothing less than annihilation in the
Fires of Love.

Let us not pray in holy half-measures nor walk
the middle path
for too long,
but pray madly, foolishly.
Let us be too ecstatic,
let us be too overwhelmed with sorrow and remorse,
let us be undone, and dismembered . . . and gladly.

Left to our own devices, ah what structures of deceit
we have created;
what battlements erected, what labyrinths woven,
what traps set for ourselves, and then
fallen into. Enough.

Let us pray dangerously—hot prayer, wet prayer, fierce prayer,
fiery prayer, improper prayer,
exuberant prayer, drunken and completely unrealistic prayer.

Let us say Yes, again and again and again.
and Yes some more.
Let us pray dangerously,

the most dangerous prayer is *Yes*.

                                        Regina Sara Ryan

Clea—La Chanson de Ma Mie'

A soft honeyed bell has tolled
Under the late autumn sky.
The road of morning—
Tall pines swathed in mist,
Standing in reverie of stone and sea.

The frosted limbs have caught the clouds
But a moment in their journey,
Becoming to your delight—
Canopies of crimson glass
Cast upon a dawn fire sea.

Later, as though locked in dream—
I watch you kneel down naked there,
Opening your arms in astonishment,
Naming it—
This human feeling that bleeds
In plain sight of the sea.

Michelle Lynn Ryan

The silence is all there is. It is the alpha and the omega. It is God's
brooding over the face of the waters; it is the blended note of the ten
thousand things, the whine of wings. You take a step in the right direction to pray to this silence, and even to address the prayer to "World."
Distinctions blur. Quit your tents. Pray without ceasing.

Annie Dillard

Oh God, whose true nature I cannot know,
You who are at once
source and substance and sustenance of my life,
I lift to you the rockhard pain I feel for this world
—and my pain dissolves into love.
I reach to the outer limits of my rational mind
to comprehend this despairing Earth
— and you call me back to my heart.

I abandon myself into my aching heart
— and it dissolves into the Heart of the Universe.
In this mystery in which all I am sure of is nothing
and all I can know is You,
give me strength; give me wisdom; and give me love.
Give me the courage and the resolve
to be the nothing that I am alone,
and to live wholly into the heart of this hurting world,
which is You.

Phoebe Phelps

With Your Light

bathe us
with the brilliance
of your light
like dew

Source unknown

When We Stumble and Find It

We all have our favorite themes,
the ones we say over and over
in a thousand different tongues.

Mine is the moment which
changed my life
forever.
Not the one I planned for
or expected, but the one which simply
happened.
It could have been a
revelation
speaking from a cloud of fire.
It could have been
a rare accomplishment, election
descending like a dove after
so many years.

It was none of these.
Merely a moment,
the one I keep returning to,
feeling along the wall for the
hidden latch

which will spring open
and reveal the undefined.

Dorothy Walters

———————

Mahakranti: The Endtime

Vespers fall across the chessboard of a convent garden.
A handful of goats upon the hillside,
Turn from shadow to dark stone.
The prayers of nuns, a phantom river seeking its course,
As the Moon also dreams of Her worlds,
The writings of stars and rivers,
And the blood tides of earth,
Returning to their point of departure.
Life and Death are but twin blossoms upon a single stem.
While morning and evening caress as middle-aged lovers,
Unknown fires rage at the world's rim.
In the distance Lord Shiva begins to sing old Rumi's song:
"Creation, Destruction!
I am dancing for them both!"

Michelle Lynn Ryan

Invocation to the Light, December 2001

On this holiday eve
with the world poised at the precipice
waiting to plunge or cross over
I call upon all the angels of mercy
who have ever shed a tear for the human race
I call upon all the guardians of peace
who have ever raised an olive branch or let fly a flock of doves
I call upon all the mystics
who have ever crossed a desert in search of the truth
I call upon all who have journeyed to the underworld
and returned with the wisdom of the dark
I call upon all the ancestral spirits who know the pain of parting the
    veil

I call upon the guardians of the four directions of the universe
O East, O South, O West, O North
help us to open our hearts to your weeping whispers
I call upon the luminous, numinous Center of the orb
O help us to embrace again the mystery of unknowing

I call upon all the animal messengers who hold the secret of oneness
I call upon all the faeries and sprites who dance in the forest
I call upon the undines, the gnomes, the sylphs, and the salamanders

the oracles of the mountains and the sages of the springs
I call upon the elves
the pookas
the djinns and the genies
the heavenly nymphs
the houris and peris
the cherubim
the seraphim
the celestial choir
the witches
the magi
the prophets
the messiah
saints and avatars
paragons and virtues
archangels in waiting
wings, haloes, and music

I call upon the three Fates
the three Graces
the nine Muses
and the seven Sisters
all the gods and goddesses

of a thousand names and guises

I call upon the Angel of the Abyss with the flame in his hand
the Angel of Memory who knows where we've been
the Angel of Truth
the Angel of Hope
the Angel of the Apocalypse who rides into the night

O come to us now
All forces of light
help us find our way through the wilderness
open our eyes to your sight

Stephanie Marohn

———————

I come in the little things
Says the Lord.

Evelyn Underhill

God Everywhere

God to enfold us, God to surround us,
God in our thinking, God in our speaking,
God in our sleeping, God in our waking,
God in our waiting, God in our hoping,
God in our minds, God in our hearts,
God in our lives, God in our deaths,
God in our ever-living souls,
God in our eternity.

Celtic oral tradition

God is present in everything.

Edith Sodergran,
Finland, 1892–1923

Beautiful One

May You,
fair as the moon
the snow and the white jasmine,
may You, seated on a white lotus
in a white sari with a vina on your lap,
may You.
glorious Goddess Sarasvati
adored by all the gods,
may You
shine your pure white light
within me.

Janine Canan

A Way In

I see in my mind a little ball of golden light.
I watch this light as it begins to grow larger and
    larger, until now it covers the entire inner
    vision of my mind.
I see within this light a beautiful temple.
I see a garden that surrounds the temple and a
    body of water that flows through the garden.
I see that the inside of the temple is lit by this
    same beautiful golden light, and I am here,
For I have been drawn here by the power and in
    the presence of God.
I dedicate my days and my relationships and
    experiences to You.
May Your Spirit, which is within me, so guide
    my thoughts, my feelings and my perceptions
    of all things
That I might grow into a happier, more peaceful,
    more loving human being.
Illumine my mind, illumine my life.
Amen.

Marianne Williamson

A Thousand Ways

The Beloved knows a thousand ways
to enter your body.

When you were young,
she sent you a lover of flesh
who stood near
to awaken your nature.

Now god is your unseen paramour
arriving without notice
on unexpected occasions.
To discover her,
turn gently, and follow your breath
to the center of your being.

Dorothy Walters

CHAPTER 10

Love

and you held me and there were no words
and there was no time and you held me
and there was only wanting and
being held and being filled with wanting
and I was nothing but letting go
and being held
and there were no words and there
needed to be no words
and there was no terror only stillness
and I was wanting nothing and
it was fullness and it was like aching for God
and it was touch and warmth and
darkness and no time and no words and we flowed
and I flowed and I was not empty
and I was given up to the dark and
in the darkness I was not lost
and the wanting was like the fullness and I could
hardly hold it and I was held and

you were dark and warm and without time and
without words and you held me

Janet Morley

Black and White Blessing

(for D., 1994)

In this one you are standing with your arms around me.
You are thirty-nine and I am nine years old, my hair long
and escaping barrettes and ponytail, wildly, finely. Your
beard and hair are dark, your glasses black-framed and very
thick, your face mostly unlined; otherwise, it's the you of
now, there, twenty-three years ago, your eyes pouring
their particular passion into the camera, your grin wide as
mine, your arms and hands bare, stained with the work of
turning fresh earth.

Behind us stands the twig of an apricot tree, too thin to
cast a shadow, and the bare yard waits for us, waits for the
lush days of mulberry and lemon and birch, of grape
arbors climbing, ping-pong games clipping the silence,
birds' nests, water lifting and collecting and planting the
light, purple agapanthus, tomatoes, corn, peas, apricots

split open in the sun, and those ladybug beetles that one
spring chose to settle into a massive five-day congregation
of feasting and flight.

I feel your snug arms around me, loose and freeing, leaving
space for me to grow beyond your shoulder, beyond, beyond,
flying over the fence with the ease and sadness,
the three-note joy of a redwing blackbird.

That day, I do not remember that particular day, but it
echoes in me anyway, with all the other ripening days, and
I hear your voice, "I will love you, no matter where you go
or what you do," and I carry that voice in me as I carry the
rhythm of skipping, as I carry the sobs and the play,
snapping towels and taste of water, ache of growth and rip
of grass, as I carry the arc of so many balls passing between
us, arm to arm, fingertip to fingertip, through sun, ocean
mist, evening of days and days, all those days packed
roundly into the stridings and restings of my long body,
into the very features of my face becoming more and more
whatever hints and guesses hovered there in the shadowed
curve of your well-used life.

Christina Hutchins

Balada

He passes by with someone else.
I have watched him go. Ever gentle was the wind,
And the road ladden with grace.
My eyes, my weary eyes
Have watched him go.

In a world of flowers, He falls in love with another.
As the thorn comes into bloom,
In a world of flowers
A song passes by.

He falls in love with another.

On the sands, at the edge of the sea,
He has kissed another.
An orange blossom moon
Rides upon the waves.
And my blood did not anoint
The ocean's vastness.

For all eternity, he will walk
With another.
There will be tranquil skies

(God begs for silence.)
For all eternity, he will walk
With another!

> Gabriela Mistral, *Chile, 1889–1957*
> *Re-creation by Michelle Lynn Ryan*

I am watching all the roads,
I am thirsting for your love,

O my beloved.

> Mahadevi, *India, twelfth century*

Between Words

The trail to the ocean is steep.
The grass we walked through, high and wet.
I hear clear wind sighing
through slender pine, silence
between your words:
that place your loneliness lives
where I want to slip under,
lie unbroken as stone.
I know where your pulse quickens

feels like water, too deep.
I know you think you might fold into yourself
as stars do, where words might not matter.
This place you won't go to let me hold you
is where I have gone.

Karen Benke

Do you ever wonder,
old lover of mine,
where so much love comes from?

I wonder this often,
because no matter how distressing the world is,
wherever I am,
there never seems to be a shortage of love.
Is this true, as well, for you?

Alice Walker

And so it came . . . it slipped itself into my heart silently, imperceptibly, and I looked at it with wonder. It was still, small; a light-blue flame trembling softly, and it had the infinite sweetness of first love, like an offering of fragrant flowers made with gentle hands, the heart full of stillness and wonder and peace.

"Love will be produced," you had said. And since then I kept wondering how it will come to me. Will it be like the voice from the Burning Bush, the voice of God as Moses heard it? Will it be like a flash of lightning out of a blue sky making the world about me a blaze of glory? Or will it be . . . Love in general, Love for everything . . . ? . . . [I]t could not be so for me, to be able to surrender completely; to sweep away all resistance, it must be big, tremendous, complete; without reserve; without limit, the conditionless, absolute, forgetting oneself.

But what I felt was not so. It was just a tender longing, so gentle, so full of infinite sweetness.

Irina Tweedie, *Russia, 1907–99*

A long time I have lived with you
And now we must be going
Separately to be together.
Perhaps I shall be the wind
To blur your smooth waters
So that you do not see your face too much.
Perhaps I shall be the star
To guide your uncertain wings
So that you have direction in the night.
Perhaps I shall be the fire
To separate your thoughts
So that you do not give up.
Perhaps I shall be the rain
To open up the earth
So that your seed may fall.
Perhaps I shall be the snow
To let your blossoms sleep
So that you may bloom in spring.
Perhaps I shall be the stream
To play a song on the rock
So that you are not alone.
Perhaps I shall be a new mountain
So that you always have a home.

Nancy Wood

First Passion

Put it down gently;
this toy is old, it has been handled
by the eager-fingered children
of all people. Each one is certain
(s)he is the first to make it breathe.
Each one is right.

Maggie Tuteur

———————————

"One must go down,
As far down as possible
To find God,"
I reasoned
with an eighteen-year-old's intensity.
And God for me meant
        forgiveness,
        faith,
        love.

Adapted from a prayer by
Anita Mathias

To Aphrodite

All the while
I prayed
Our night would last
Twice as long.

Sappho, *Greece,*
seventh century, B.C.E.

Who Will Teach Me Now?

O, commemorate me where there is water—Patrick Kavanagh

Wind tosses the waves into white caps,
moves the clouds. A moon-high tide
takes me along the estuary, to a place with sand.

I lay a towel down, unpack the bag
with a live lobster, a white candle,
and the ceramic box holding your ashes.

A sailboat across the bay, then two terns diving:
I'd forgotten how to sit still. I light the candle,
lift the cover: somehow I hear laughter.

I wait, you don't move in the wind.
So I unbind the lobster's claws,
then lift the box spilling some of the ashes

on his back. I watch him scuttle off into the water
vanishing with you into the seaweed and eel grass.
Happy day for you, don't get caught this time.

I empty the box above the high-tide line
believing I could always find this exact spot
and you among the shells and rocks.

I beg mercy for I'd forgotten
how I love this hard place,
where you taught me how talk to God

anywhere. Walking until there was no place for feet,
I kneel there, dip my fingers
and touch seawater to my forehead,

my heart and each shoulder.
I hear you singing loud and off key.

Anne-Marie Madden Irwin

The Soul in Love

As the fish swims freely
in the vastness of the seas,
as the bird soars boldly
in the vastness of the air,
so I feel my spirit roaming free
in the depths and heights and immensity
of love.

Beatrice of Nazareth, *Brabant*
(Netherlands and Belgium), c.1200–68

My Book Was Begun in Love

My book was begun in love,
and must also end in love.
For there is nothing
so wise or holy,
so beautiful or so strong,
and so perfect as love.

Mechtild of Magdeburg,
Germany, c.1212–82

You Have Come, My Beloved

You have come, my beloved,
The clouds are gone.
The wind is silent.
The sun appears,
and the trees are green.

Adapted from a poem by
Tinh Thuy, Vietnam

No Words At All, Just Love*

I will go on. I know that the states of Nearness will increase, will become more permanent but also that the state of separation will become more painful, more lonely the nearer I come to Reality. This I cannot avoid; it belongs to this school of training. And it does not matter anymore. The memory of nearness to you will remain and will give me strength to go on. I know I go back to a life of fire; for you, my dear, before accepting me, you told me what to expect. And I said, Yes! and sealed my destiny. I know health will fail me sometimes, I know I will be burned, and it will not matter, for always, always, I will remember that I belong...and that will give me strength to go on....

---

* Written shortly after the death of her spiritual teacher

Last night I prayed but there were no words...just love, immense, no end of it. I have not prayed for anything lately. There is stillness. A strange happiness, but no words at all. Just love, and love, and love, non-ending, and infinitely serene.

Irina Tweedie, *Russia, 1907–99*

Mira Speaks to Her Lord

Mira says:
Dark One,
Come to my bedroom.

I've scattered fresh buds
on the couch,
perfumed my body.

Birth after birth
I am your servant,
sleep only with you.

Mirabai,
India, 1498–c.1550

A Dying Grandfather's Prayer

I will watch over you,
I will bless those who bless you.

Rachel Naomi Remen

———————

To Be an Island in the Sea

And now,
may kindly Columba guide you
to be an island in the sea,
a hill on the shore,
a star in the night,
a staff for the weak.
Amen.

Scotland, Gaelic oral tradition,
first millennium?

———————

In this still moment, Lord,
I thank You for this second chance.
I accept all that has gone before.
I pledge myself to this new love.
Help me to honor our experiences in the past,

and all our differences.
Help me to trust that we have learned from our mistakes
And will enrich our lives
Together and apart,
learning from one another,
learning from sorrow and joy,
from sickness and health,
from acquiring and letting go.
Thank you for all this love.
Thank you for all that went before,
the happiness and the pain.
Thank you for this blessing.
May it be the sacred center of our lives
For the rest of our days.

Anonymous,
New Zealand

Cold

The white floor, the white back splash
give back light to the honey-colored
cabinets and the scatter rugs.

My blue kettle over a blue flame
almost to the boil, the cat insists
on canned food, her Siamese cry.

Your letter arrived yesterday,
air-mail edge, Mexican stamps.
Written in Spanish, I tried to find

my way through the *caminos*
but stumbled on the reflexives,
lost you to the subjunctive.

Why didn't you call? I want to climb
into your voice. I'd have told you
how the sky dropped fifteen inches

of snow yesterday. How I dug out
the cars, a pathway to the mailbox,
a labyrinth in the garden. Each filled

shovel heavier than the last, until my arms
could no longer feel your absence.
The ache moved out from my chest

to shoulders, hipbone and thighs.
With your letter laid down, beneath my pillow,
I slept without remembered dreams.

Anne-Marie Madden Irwin

I Am My Beloved's

I am My Beloved's
And he is mine.
Come my beloved,
Let us go forth into the field;
And lodge in the villages.
Let us go up early to the vineyards;
Let us see whether the vine has budded,
Whether the grape has opened,
And the pomegranates are in bloom;
There will I give thee my love.
The mandrakes give forth fragrance,
And at the door are all manner of precious fruits, new and old
Which I have laid up for thee, O my beloved.

Anonymous woman's prayer
from the Song of Songs 7.10–13

All She Needed That Day

Email to my husband

The nurse held her at the kitchen sink
while I shampooed your mother's hair,
I wanted to color it for her.

Your mother told me over coffee,
when she was young she did too much,
her heart raced. She was running the factory
with your father, four children and politics.

When a doctor ordered her to slow down
she asked how and he replied,
What is it you like that you're not doing?

She wished she had time for her hair.
So he wrote her a prescription:
Once a week go to the hairdresser.
Forty years she followed his order.

With her head in my hands,
her closed eyes sat deep in their sockets,
and knew she was dying.

But as suds swirled down the drain, we laughed,
a giggle women share in kitchens
out of male earshot, when children sleep.

She sat down, her chest heaving
she leaned into me, a towel swaddled her head—
you should have seen her face, just then.

Anne-Marie Madden Irwin

————————

To what shall I liken you, Lord?
to the dove that feeds its little ones,
to a tender mother who nourishes her child.

Mariam Baouardy, France, 1846–78

INDEX OF
AUTHORS AND SOURCES

INDEX OF TITLES
OR FIRST LINES

Ballantine Books, New York, NY, for an excerpt from "Letting Go" by Stephanie Kaza in *The Attentive Heart: Conversation with Trees,* copyright © 1993 by Stephanie Kaza.

Beacon Press, Boston, MA, for an excerpt from *Voices of the Matriarchs* edited by Chava Weissler, copyright © 1998 by Chava Weissler; for an excerpt from "Prayer" by Lisa Colt, copyright © by Elizabeth H. Colt, from *Claiming the Spirit Within: A Sourcebook of Women's Poetry* edited by Marilyn Sewell, copyright ©1996 by Marilyn Sewell.

Bloodaxe Books, Tarset, Northumberland, England, for an excerpt from "I Taught Myself to Live Simply" by Anna Akhmatova from *Selected Poems* by Anna Akhmatova translated by Richard McKane, copyright © 1989 by Richard McKane.

The Buddhist Peace Fellowship, Berkeley, CA, for "Metta Prayer" by Maylie Scott in *Turning Wheel: the Journal of Socially Engaged Buddhism*

Calyx Books, Corvallis, OR, for an excerpt from "The Power In My Mother's Arms" by Florence Weinberger from *Women and Aging: An Anthology by Women* edited by Jo Alexander et al, copyright © 1986 by Calyx Books.

"Calyx: A Journal of Art and Literature" Vol. 14, No. 3 (Summer, 1993) for an excerpt from "The Meaning of Bones" by Megan Sexton.

Janine Canan for "Beautiful One," and translation of "The Stars" by Simone Weil.

Jonathan Cape Ltd., London, England, for "You have made me so rich" from *The Diaries of Etty Hillesum 1941–1943* by Etty Hillesum, translation of Otto Pomerans copyright © 1983 by Otto Pomerans.

Christian Aid, London, England, for "For Victims of War and Refugees" by Janet Morley from *Companions of God* by Janet Morley, copyright © 1994 by Janet Morley.

Christianity and Crisis, March 3, 1986, for kind permission to reprint "Listen" by Linda Lancione Moyer, copyright © *Christianity and Crisis* 537 W. 121st St., New York, NY 10027.

Harvard University Press, Cambridge, MA, The Belknap Press of Harvard University Press for "I saw no Way" from *The Poems of Emily Dickinson*, edited by Tomas H. Johnson, copyright © 1951, 1955, 1979 by the President and Fellows of Harvard College.

"Heartbeats: Networking Women, Developing World, and Minority Artists," A Ministry of the Sisters of the Humility of Mary, 20015 Detroit Rd., Cleveland, OH 22116, for the series of five prayers, "Blessed Are You" by Margaret Cessna, H. M. For a catalogue, e-mail at Heartbt@en.com. Tel. 440–356–8601. Reprinted by kind permission of Heartbeats.

Pat Corrick Hinton, for an excerpt from "All You Clear and Shimmering Waters," in *Prayers for Growing and Other Pains*, HarperCollins Publishers, Inc., copyright © 1994 by Pat Corrick Hinton.

Jane Hirshfield, for kind permission to reprint "Bonsai," "Theology," and "The Monk Stood Beside a Wheelbarrow."

Hohm Press, Prescott, AZ, for "A Thousand Ways," "When We Stumble and Find It," "Order of Melchizedek," and "What Is Happening" from *Marrow of Flame: Poems of the Spiritual Journey* by Dorothy Walters, copyright © 2000 by Dorothy Walters; and for "Bodhi" and "Dangerous Prayers" from *Praying Dangerously: Radical Reliance on God* by Regina Sara Ryan, copyright © 2001 by Regina Sara Ryan.

Alicia Hokanson, for "This Island, this Season."

"iris: A Journal About Women," Vol. 13 (Summer, 1993), Charlottesville, VA, for "The Boston School of Cooking Cookbook" by Rhona McAdam, copyright © 1993 by Iris.

Jeevan-Dhara Ashram Society, Jaihari Khal, Garhwal Himalayas, "O Lord, One tiny bit of water," by Ishpriya, RSCJ, in *Kalkalnadini (The Singing of the Stream)*, copyright © 1984 by Ishpriya, RSCJ.

Lyn Klug, for excerpts from *Soul Weavings: A Gathering of Women's Prayers* edited by Lyn Klug, copyright © 1996 by Lyn Klug.

Liveright Publishing Company, for "A Zen Prayer for Preparing a Meal: How to Stuff a Pepper " by Nancy Willard from *Carpenter of the Sun: Poems by Nancy Willard*, copyright © 1974 by Nancy Willard. Used by permission of W. W. Norton & Company, Inc.

Medical Mission Sisters, for "God Our Mother, Living Water."

Marion Milner, for "From Self-Consciousness to Happiness."

New Directions Publishing Corp., for an excerpt from "The Well" in *Breathing the Water* by Denise Levertov, copyright © 1982, 1987 by Denise Levertov.

New Society Publishers, for an excerpt from "Prayer" from *A Shallow Pool of Time* by Fran Peavey, copyright ©1988 by Fran Peavey.

W. W. Norton, New York, NY, for "Pastoral" by Rita Dove from *Grace Notes*, copyright © 1989 by Rita Dove; for an excerpt from *Wise Women* by Susan Cahill, copyright © 1996 by Susan Cahill; for an excerpt from *Collected Poems1930–1973* by May Sarton, copyright ©1974 by May Sarton.

Perennial (An Imprint of HarperCollins*Publishers*), New York, NY, for an excerpt from *The Antelope Wife* by Louise Erdrich, copyright © 1998 by Louise Erdrich.

Rabbinical Assembly of America and United Synagogue of America, New York, NY, for an excerpt from *Siddur Sim Shalom: A Prayer Book for Shabbat, Festivals, and Weekdays* edited and translated by Jules Harlow, copyright © 1985 by Jules Harlow.

Riverhead Books (division of G. P. Putnam's Sons; Penguin Putnam, Inc.), New York, NY, for "the Holy may speak to you" in *My Grandfather's Blessings: Stories of Refuge, Strength, and Belonging* by Rachel Naomi Remen, M.D., copyright © 2000 by Rachel Naomi Remen.

Michelle Lynn Ryan, for permission to reprint "*Clea—La Chanson de Ma Mie,'*" Mahakranti: The Endtime," and her re-creation of Gabriela Mistral's poem, "*Balada*" from *From the Minarets of the Heart: Selected Poems 1968–2001* by Michelle Lynn Ryan, copyright © 2002 by Michelle Lynn Ryan.

Scarlet Tanager Books, Oakland, CA, for "you," "Mother of Mothers," and "to dance at your daughter's wedding" from *Red Clay Is Talking* by Naomi Ruth Lowinsky, copyright © 2000 by Naomi Ruth Lowinsky.

M.P.A. Schaeffer for *Ti Prego*, copyright © 2002 by M.P.A. Schaeffer.

Joanne Seltzer, for "Women Who Light Lives."

Shambhala Publications, Inc., Boston, MA, for an excerpt from *Heaven's Face Thinly Veiled: A Book of Spiritual Writing by Women* edited by Sarah Anderson, copyright © 1996 by Sarah Anderson.

SPCK publishers, London, England, for "and you held me" and "For the Darkness of Waiting" from *All Desires Known: Inclusive Prayers for Worship and Meditation* by Janet Morley, copyright © 1992 by Janet Morley.

The Golden Sufi Center, Inverness, CA, for an excerpt from *Daughter of Fire: A Diary of a Spiritual Training with a Sufi Master* by Irina Tweedie, copyright © 1986 by The Golden Sufi Center UK Charitable Trust.

United Reformed Church, England, for "Learning to Grow" by Kate Compston from *Encounters, The Prayer Handbook*, copyright © 1988 by the United Reformed Church.

University of California Press, Berkeley, CA, for Fragment #46 "Thank you, my dear," from *Sappho: A New Translation* tr. by Mary Bernard, copyright ©1958 by Mary Barnard. Reprinted with permission of University of California Press.

Marianne Williamson for "A Way In."

Nancy Wood for "A long time I have lived with you" from *Many Winters,* Doubleday & Co., a division of Bantam Doubleday Dell Publishing Group, Inc., copyright © 1974 by Nancy Wood.

Zodervan Publishers, for "and you held me" by Janet Morley, "Lord of Healing" by Alison Pepper, "For Victims of War and Refugees" by Janet Morley, and "Open our eyes to see our own part" by Angela Ashwin from *The Book of a Thousand Prayers*, compiled by Angela Ashwin, copyright © 1996 by Angela Ashwin; permission of Zodervan Publishers, Grand Rapids, MI.

ABOUT THE EDITOR

Mary Ford-Grabowsky is an award-wining writer, teacher, and scholar with a specialty in the world's mystical traditions. She taught in the religious studies department at Regis College and was editor-in-chief of the international journal *Fellowship in Prayer* for which she received the World Council of Church's ecumenical award for distinguished service in interfaith work. Her publications include many academic and inspirational articles and six books, among them the highly acclaimed *Sacred Voices: Essential Women's Wisdom Through the Ages* (HarperSan-Francisco, 2002), a One Spirit Book Club selection. The recipient of a master of divinity degree and a doctorate in theology and spirituality from Princeton Theological Seminary, she also studied at the National University of Mexico and the University of Bonn, Germany, conducting research in eight languages: German, French, Spanish, Italian, Latin, Greek, and Hebrew, in addition to English. Ford-Grabowsky has extensive experience on the East and West coasts as a lecturer, workshop leader, and radio and TV speaker, and today is actively engaged in research on women's writings in the world's religious and mystical traditions. She is married and the mother of a daughter.